Assessment in Physical Education

Assessment has widely been acknowledged as a central element of institutional education, shaping curriculum and pedagogy in powerful ways and representing a critical reference point in political, professional and public debates about educational achievement and policy directions. Within physical education there remains significant debate regarding the subject knowledge, skills and understandings that should be assessed and in what ways and at what points in education this should occur.

Divided into ... ts, *Assessment in Physical Education* makes an important contributio ... understanding of the sociocultural issues associated with assessmen ... al education, both in terms of its systemic development and at the level ... gic relations between physical education teachers and their students. ... readers with an insightful critique and theoretically informed ideas ... king assessment policies and practices in physical education.

This book w ... interest to advanced students and researchers in physical educati ... uth sport studies, as well as those involved in initial teacher educati ... cher professional development.

Peter Hay is a ... turer in the School of Human Movement Studies, The University o ... nd, Australia. His work has focused on assessment practices and po ... d beyond the field of physical education and the social constructi ... ties in institutional education settings.

Dawn Penney is ... of Physical Education and Sport Pedagogy in the Department of ... eisure Studies in the Faculty of Education at the University of W ... ealand. Dawn is recognised internationally for her work in policy a ... development in Health and Physical Education.

rned

Routledge studies in physical education and youth sport

Series Editor: David Kirk, University of Bedfordshire, UK

The Routledge Studies in Physical Education and Youth Sport series is a forum for the discussion of the latest and most important ideas and issues in physical education, sport and active leisure for young people across school, club and recreational settings. The series presents the work of the best well-established and emerging scholars from around the world, offering a truly international perspective on policy and practice. It aims to enhance our understanding of key challenges, to inform academic debate, and to have a high impact on both policy and practice, and is thus an essential resource for all serious students of physical education and youth sport.

Also available in this series

Assessment in Physical Education

A sociocultural perspective

Peter Hay and Dawn Penney

Routledge
Taylor & Francis Group

LONDON AND NEW YORK

First published 2013
by Routledge
2 Park Square, Milton Park, Abingdon, Oxfordshire OX14 4RN

Simultaneously published in the USA and Canada
by Routledge
711 Third Avenue, New York, NY 10017

First issued in paperback 2014

Routledge is an imprint of the Taylor & Francis Group, an informa business

British Library Cataloguing in Publication Data
A catalogue record for this book is available from the British Library

Library of Congress Cataloging in Publication Data
Hay, Peter.
Assessment in physical education : a sociocultural perspective / Peter Hay,
Dawn Penney.
p. cm. -- (Routledge studies in physical education and youth sport)
1. Physical education and training--Evaluation. 2. Physical education and
training--Social aspects. 3. Physical education and training--Study and
teaching. 4. Physical education and training--Curricula. I. Penney, Dawn,
1966- II. Title.
GV362.H35 2012
613.71--dc23
2012010475

ISBN13: 978-0-415-60272-3 (hbk)
ISBN13: 978-1-138-79575-4 (pbk)

Typeset in Times
by Taylor & Francis Books

Contents

1　Introduction

Over the past 20 years the significance of assessment has been increasingly recognised in the field of physical education. Such recognition has been evidenced by efforts to theorise and conceptualise assessment in physical education (e.g. Hay and Penney, 2009), as well as proliferating reports of specific research endeavours focusing on the impact of assessment on students and physical education practices (e.g. Annerstedt and Larsson, 2010; MacPhail and Halbert, 2010; Redelius and Hay, 2009) and the dissemination of assessment practice initiatives from around the world (e.g. Blomqvist *et al.*, 2005; Nadeau *et al.*, 2007; Oslin, 2003; Thorburn, 2007). The basis for this burgeoning interest has been mixed. Some have advocated the practice of assessment because of its potential contributions to effective pedagogy and student learning (Veal, 1995; Hay, 2006), while others have noted the importance of assessment and accountability to the standing of physical education within local, national and international curriculum settings (Hardman and Marshall, 2000). Meanwhile, past research efforts have highlighted that within the physical education community there are those who view assessment with a degree of suspicion, questioning whether the intentions and practices of assessment may in fact be counter to the nature, purpose and potential of the subject itself (Kneer, 1986; Matanin and Tannehill, 1994).

It is important that the international physical education community continues to broaden as well as deepen its interest in, and discussions about, assessment in and beyond the subject, given the significance of assessment in education more broadly. In this regard, assessment is arguably one of the most influential facets of contemporary education practice. At every level within and between education systems, from local schools right through to contexts of global systemic comparisons, assessment expectations, practices and outcomes have significantly shaped what is taught in schools, why it is taught, and how it is taught. This has perhaps been no better exemplified than in the impact of the Programme for International Student Assessment (PISA), developed by the Organisation for Economic Cooperation and Development (OECD), on education interests and practices internationally and locally. This standardised assessment programme, developed and administered by an economic organisation, has precipitated unprecedented curriculum and assessment reforms across the member nations of the OECD. In Australia, for example, socio-political concerns over the relative decline in PISA achievement outcomes of Australian students have fuelled significant political will for curriculum and assessment reform across the country. Practically, this political will has been manifest in the development and implementation of a national curriculum and a national standardised testing regime. It was not coincidental that the subjects developed in the primary phase of the national curriculum included English, Mathematics, Science and History, given three of the four subjects' direct connection with the primary content foci of PISA. The National Assessment Program – Literacy and Numeracy (NAPLAN) has been similarly focused (in terms of content and structure) to reflect the content and interests of international comparative measures in an endeavour to ensure that Australia assumes and maintains a prominent international standing in relation to the quality of its education system. This national quest for global education competitiveness has had a direct impact on the curriculum development practices and pedagogies of many schools right across the country, where local school curricular endeavours have been reprioritised to focus more heavily on literacy and numeracy as well as provide time for regular NAPLAN 'practice' to ensure that the achievement standards at each school are competitive within the national system.

For physical education, the implications of these reform responses to an international assessment programme are compelling. In the Australian example, health and physical education was not initially considered a priority for national curriculum development and was only eventually nominated by the Australian Curriculum, Assessment Reporting Authority (ACARA) as a focus for development and implementation as part of a 'Phase 3' initiative following considerable lobbying from invested stakeholders such as universities, health-affiliated professional organisations and sporting bodies. Clearly, the initial absence of commitment to physical education in schools and then the phased introduction of other curriculum areas served to convey the government's perceptions of the relative value of subjects to students' educational experiences. The increasing significance of NAPLAN to the standing of schools and specific funding arrangements has also impacted on the time that schools provide for content and activities other than those specifically captured in the systemic testing regime. In numerous cases this has resulted in the truncation, and in some cases cessation, of substantial (health and) physical education programmes.

A sociocultural perspective

Clearly, in order to understand assessment practices in physical education, we must be cognisant of the influence of assessment beyond the subject. Subjects and the assessment practices that occur within them do not operate independently of, or unaffected by, the systemic environments in which they are situated.

Assessment is complex and it is not so much the practicalities or technicalities of assessment that imbue it with its complexity, but rather the fact that its social origins and consequences are so diverse, messy and influential. Constraining one's focus to the practical and technical elements of assessment carries the potential to overlook these significant factors and thus may undermine the potential efficacy of the practice itself. As Gipps (1999) reminded us, 'decisions about even apparently technical matters are influenced by political and ideological considerations' (p. 355). With this in mind it can be seen that, in order to optimise the practice of assessment in physical education, the basis for the practice and social dynamics of the assessment context need to be first understood.

A sociocultural perspective on assessment provides the breadth of focus necessary to comprehend the external and internal factors affecting assessment practices in physical education as well as the consequences of those practices for the subject and its key stakeholders. Critically, this perspective also draws attention to the fact that assessment is fundamentally a *social activity*. Assessments are required by people, developed by people, implemented by people and performed by people and have implications for people right across education systems. For this reason Gipps (1999) proposed that assessment can only be properly understood if the social, cultural, economic and political contexts of its operation are taken into account. Accordingly, a sociocultural perspective on assessment orients our focus to these social and cultural factors informing the conceptions and implementations of assessment as well as the impact that these conceptions and implementations have on the macro- and microsocieties to which they are directed.

Failing to recognise the social and cultural inputs and outcomes of assessment can lead to some significant and potentially problematic assumptions about assessment. Consider, for example, the meritocratic assumptions that underpin many large-scale systemic measures of students' scholastic performances. On the basis of these assumptions, the outcomes of what are declared to be *technically valid measures* of defined capacity are believed to reflect the innate abilities and efforts of the candidates involved. The implications, in light of the widely reported achievement disparities between students in higher and lower socio-economic contexts (e.g. Connolly, 2006; Dunne and Gazeley, 2008; Knapp and Woolverton, 2004; Teese, 2000; Teese and Polesel, 2003), are that students from lower socio-economic areas are less intelligent or 'able', or generally more lazy. What is overlooked, which a sociocultural perspective directs our attention to, is the fact that these measures are written or controlled by middle-class education bureaucrats, and that children from lower socio-economic areas are less likely to have access to the same social and cultural resources as their higher socio-economic counterparts. Failing to challenge or question the meritocratic assumptions of systemic assessment regimes can have the impact of narrowing the real and perceived educational and vocational advancement opportunities of those with the least economic, cultural and social resources (Connolly and Healy, 2004; McLeod and Yates,

2006), while those from higher socio-economic areas potentially enjoy more optimistic educational futures.

We see then that there is something of a *critical* edge to the sociocultural perspective we are pursuing in this book. By critical, we do not mean that we view assessment as inherently bad or good. Neither are we assuming a classical critical inquiry position such as those posed by Kincheloe and McLaren (1994) or Popkewitz (1999), where the intention is to uncover inherent social inequities and injustices produced through practices or technologies of social control. Rather, our view acknowledges that any social endeavour or practice has *consequences* for those engaged within or by the endeavour and that these consequences are disproportionate in their effects. Again, this does not render assessment fundamentally problematic, but it does mean that it is important to consider what these effects might be, how the effects are distributed and what factors may contribute to these effects.

A critical perspective also draws attention to the manifestations and outcomes of power and control. As Penney and Evans have reminded us, 'all pedagogical relations invoke power relations; there is no instruction without regulation, no pedagogy divorced of control' (2004, p. 5). In many ways this is obvious in assessment practices, as the power of the teacher is manifest in their responsibility and authority to make judgements on students regarding certain facets of educational capacity. Implicit in the authority and work of assessment is the power to confer on students symbols representing the quality of their capacities in relation to constructed measures. Not only do the teachers make the decisions, but more often than not their perceptions, values and beliefs are significant in the formulation of those decisions. In the construction, implementation and marking of assessment pieces, the control of the teacher is evident in the selection of the mode of communication (physical performance, written piece, oral presentation, etc.), the response sequence, the criteria on which judgements are made and the assigning of grades to students (Bernstein, 1996). In contrast, the limited recourse of students to change the parameters of the assessment, avoid being assessed and challenge the judgements and their consequences, are all stark reminders of the comparatively weaker power and control states of the students. Of course, power and control operate within schools beyond the practices of assessment, and yet it is the outcomes of assessment that influence the students' own power within the school and beyond it. Furthermore, as we will develop later, assessment expectations and outcomes for students and schools are important factors in the operation of power and control within and across the whole system.

Assessment as a message system

These brief examples of the operations of power and control in relation to assessment draw attention to the role that assessment performs in *communicating value* within an education system. In this regard, we can view assessment as operating as a message system. In describing the forms and control of knowledge production and reproduction in schools, Bernstein argued that the selection, classification, transmission and assessment of educational knowledge could be viewed as occurring through the three inter-related message systems of pedagogy, curriculum and evaluation (or in our current vernacular, assessment) (Bernstein, 1971). Notably, Bernstein proposed that the messages and their communication were the 'consequence of the interactional practice within a context' (1990, p. 23), further substantiating our observations of the social bases of assessment in all its forms and purposes. In relation to the critical facets of our sociocultural perspective, Bernstein's identification of message systems provokes thought about the nature and consequences of particular systemic messages for schools, subjects, teachers and students operating within education systems.

Just as international and national systemic assessment imperatives have an influence on the extent to which subjects such as physical education are valued, assessment practices within subjects communicate values and shape the practices and experiences of key stakeholders therein. Consider that the intention to assess 'something' implies that the 'something' is worthwhile finding out about. Where some facets of a subject are assessed and others are not, by implication a distinction is made between the relative values of those facets. Similarly, assessment provides a mechanism for assigning value (in the form of grades) to those students who demonstrate the possession of valued knowledge and skills in a valued manner. The learning consequence of engagement with this message of value ascription and representation could be conceived of as the development of one's perception of value within and of the subject. At a macro level, as we noted in relation to the impact of PISA on curriculum reform, this is evident in relation to the value of subjects themselves. Recognition within the physical education community of the significance of assessment to the value of subject areas is exemplified in Rink and Mitchell's statement that 'one unintended outcome of the standards, assessment and accountability movement is that any program [or subject] not included in high stakes state level assessment, for all practical purposes, does not "count"' (2002, p. 209), and Hardman and Marshall's equation of the lower status of physical education internationally with a 'lack of official assessment' (2000, p. 15).

The common thread concerning assessment beyond and within physical education is the communication of value. This is a key function of assessment and provides a significant basis, in current educational environments, for a peculiar mode of administration where curricular and pedagogical value is communicated via official assessment expectations. The degree of compliance with these expectations within the system is determined by the assessment outcomes of those being subjected to the assessment processes. Notwithstanding the potential negative consequences of pedagogic actions of the message systems (from the macro through to a micro level), recognising the mechanisms through which knowledge is selected, transmitted and assessed also helps us to understand how to *optimise the transmission of valued messages*. That is, the inter-relatedness of the message systems, as well as the fact that the communication of the messages occurs as a consequence of interactional practices in schools (Bernstein, 1990), is important to note as they highlight that effective educational work in schools *depends on the alignment and coherence* of the three message systems (Penney *et al.*, 2009) and a certain quality of stakeholder engagement within the system.

There has been much written in physical education literature concerning the messages communicated through curriculum and pedagogy, but comparatively less consideration given to the message system of assessment. This is not ignoring the increasing number of articles written about assessment techniques, but rather describing the absence of reference to assessment as a message system, or the effects of the system on physical education and its participants. We believe that this is quite an oversight, given Broadfoot's observation that 'assessment procedures are so closely bound up with the legitimisation of particular educational practices' (1996, p. 87) such that assessment may be the most important of the three message systems.

Clarifying assessment

Having drawn attention to the operation of assessment as a message system, let us take a moment to clarify the language of our own 'messages' in this book. Sadler (2005) noted that discussions about assessment were notoriously hampered by semantic differences in the definition of terms and their theoretical and practical employment in education literature. International disparities in the employment and recognition of assessment terms are particularly notable. For example, the term 'authentic assessment' has particular currency in Europe, Australia and New Zealand; however, 'performance assessment' is the preferred term in the USA. Some would even argue that one or the other is a superior iteration of the intention towards learning-oriented and ecologically valid assessment, a claim that would no doubt be strongly countered by others. We take the view that such debates over what are largely semantic issues are unlikely to be resolved and offer little value for understanding and promoting productive assessment in physical education. Rather than attempting to comprehend and account for all the possible nuanced differences in assessment terms, for the purpose of communicating a sociocultural perspective on assessment we will provide some clarity on the terms that we will be using throughout this book. In this respect we do not view our clarifications as globally definitive, but anticipate that they will provide readers with a reasonable entry into the theoretical and conceptual offerings we are making.

Let us begin by proposing a definition of assessment itself. We employ the term 'assessment' in a comprehensive manner to include *any action of information collection within education settings that is initiated for the purpose of making some interpretive judgements about students*. This definition is deliberately broad and encompasses official and formal measures such as high-stakes standardised tests right through to the day-to-day informal judgements that teachers make on the learning states and progress of their students. The central features of our definition are *collecting information* and *making interpretations*. Implicit in these two foundational elements are the assumptions that information will be collected in education settings via various methods and that the information collected will be interpreted in different ways depending upon the *purpose* of collecting the information and the associated way in which the information is used.

Broadfoot and Black (2004) proposed that the purposes and imperatives of assessment are essentially underpinned by the policy and practice contexts of the information use. Similarly, Hay (2006) noted that 'decisions concerning who is to be assessed, what is to be assessed, and how the assessment is to occur reflect social, cultural and political contexts and differ according to changes in context' (p. 313). Accordingly, assessment serves and has served many different purposes in education, including providing a basis for selection into higher levels of study or vocational avenues; certification of standards of learning and attainment; reporting to students and parents; systemic accountability for meeting curriculum and policy directives; motivation for student engagement in learning experiences; diagnosis of learning or comprehension deficiencies; and feedback for informing ongoing learning. In many cases these purposes overlap (as exemplified by the relationship between certification and selection), adding to the complexity and messiness of assessment. In order, then, to analyse assessment practices and their outcomes it is helpful to apply some general classifications to the multiple purposes of assessment. With this in mind, we propose that the varied purposes of assessment can be broadly categorised within two main endeavours: *accountability* and *learning*.

Focusing our attention on accountability, it is necessary to specify what we mean by educational accountability. Conventionally and popularly, accountability is viewed as an operational feature of education systems where those functionaries operating at the lower levels of the system give an account, often through student assessment outcomes, for the enactment of certain directives (such as curriculum expectations) to those who delivered the directives (Ranson, 2003). However, we view this feature of education systems as only one element of accountability. Assessment for accountability is assessment that provides opportunity for an *account of learning*. That is, the information collected through assessment is used to inform others of learning and learning quality (or performance). Others have described this purpose of assessment as 'assessment of learning'. However, we prefer the term 'accountability', as it implies a specific and intended communication of that assessed learning through, for example, report cards, certificates, league tables, selection processes, etc. We could say that it is assessment that 'counts' for something and is therefore 'accounted'. This purpose and form of assessment has also been described as 'summative' assessment. In relation to our categories of purposes, rather than summative assessment operating as a purpose in its own right, we view it as tasks or programmes that provide or contribute to an account of learning.

At this point it is necessary to highlight an often overlooked or misunderstood facet of assessment. Assessment and the assigning of grades to students' work or on their report cards are commonly viewed as synonymous. However, we do not share this view and argue that the conflation of these two processes is a key facilitator of the problematic consequences of assessment and the undermining of its potential benefits to students and the subject more generally. The distinction is clear when we consider that assessment involves the collection and interpretation of information, while grading represents a summary of that interpretation, communicated via a symbol. Grading is a means of *communicating* (albeit in a clumsy manner) an account; it is not the means of *arriving* at the account. With this distinction in mind, we can envisage a physical education devoid of grades, but in which assessment is a central feature of the educative endeavours of the subject. In fact we advocate grading-free assessment in primary school physical education so that the performative consequences of assessment on students' perceptions of themselves and their engagement in physical education are not unduly influential, and so that the learning benefits of assessment can be optimised. In the secondary school context, for the systemic reasons we explore in Chapter 3, we recognise the importance of grading to the situation and acceptance of physical education within broader school and system practices. Nevertheless, even in the secondary school context it is important that the distinction between the processes of assessment and grading are understood by teachers and students as part of their *assessment literacy* (see Chapter 6).

Hayes *et al.* nominate assessment as 'perhaps the most maligned aspect of the teaching and learning processes in schools' (2006, p. 82) because of the broadly identified negative outcomes of assessment for accountability and as a consequence of the blurred understandings of the relationship between assessment and grading. These reported negative outcomes have included, for example, the inordinate professional pressure placed on teachers to achieve high cohort-performance standards that Ball (2003), drawing on the work of Lyotard (1984), described as the 'terrors of performativity'; shifts in school foci from the pursuit of educational or learning substance to optimising achievement symbols and representations of quality; and the inordinate effects on the self-efficacy and mental well-being of many students.

Both in reaction to these negative consequences and as a result of developing theories of learning, assessment has been widely positioned as serving the purpose of promoting student *learning*. Variously describing it as 'formative assessment', 'educative assessment' and 'assessment for learning', advocates of this purpose have argued that assessment tasks and outcomes can inform, support and promote student learning. There are two key facets of such a view. The first is the most widely recognised formative potential of assessment (Black and Wiliam, 1998, 2006, 2009). In this regard, Black and Wiliam, arguably the two most notable protagonists of assessment for learning internationally, proposed that 'the quality of interactive feedback is a critical feature in determining the quality of learning activity, and is therefore a central feature of pedagogy' (2006, p. 100). The view of assessment as providing information for learners and ongoing learning is generally described as an elaboration of constructivist theories of learning (Shepard, 2000; Taras, 2002). Broadly, we can suggest that constructivists take the view that learning occurs as a result of interactions between learners and instructors, and within contexts, and that students actively appropriate and adapt new knowledge in relation to former understandings and cognitive structures. Moreover, constructivist theories recognise that learning is not a passive process of knowledge transmission. Rather, it is a complex process, dependent upon students' previous knowledge, the mode of learning (e.g. kinaesthetic, visual, auditory), the context and the task (Rovai, 2004).

The second key facet of assessment that has a particular learning purpose is the view that the assessment experience itself can promote valued learning. Earl (2003) has described this as assessment 'as' learning and argued that students learn through participating in assessment tasks and that this potential is as important as the information that is collected on the students' capacities once the assessment task or programme is completed. Earl's view has a notable ontological resonance with other conceptual efforts towards enriching the assessment experience for students, such as *authentic assessment* and *performance assessment*. These forms of assessment require students to demonstrate and effectively and elaborately communicate an in-depth understanding of subject matter (Herrington *et al.*, 2003). More specifically, they provide assessable learning experiences that are *connected* to the world in which the students live or work (Shepard, 2000). That is, the learning experiences that form the medium for information gathering have application and meaning for students' lives and are not abstract or disassociated. The tasks should also require students to demonstrate a *range* of knowledges and processes in a manner beyond the passive recall of content.

Continuing with our definitional clarifications, let us comment on the nomenclature we have chosen to use in this book to identify or represent the subject area. Internationally there are variations in the titles and associated curricular content of (health) and physically oriented subjects. For example, the learning area is variously titled Health and Physical Education (e.g. Australia, New Zealand), Physical Education and Health (e.g. Sweden), Physical Education (e.g. UK, USA, Finland), etc. We have chosen to use the term physical education, because of its consistent representation in titles of international education systems and because of its widely and historically recognised representation in curricula across the world. We certainly are not seeking to limit the scope of curriculum possibilities associated with the area as we believe, for example, that health education is an important entitlement for all students. What we do believe is important and captured well in the term 'physical education' is the unique place of *movement* in the learning associated with the subject. In terms of assessment, however, the principles we attend to in this book are not constrained to the psychomotor domain but are tenable across the range of curricular representations and constitutions (including health education) of the subject area. Indeed, while we are particularly focusing on physical education, we argue that the sociocultural assessment principles advocated in this book are relevant in any curriculum or educational setting.

Where to from here?

The purpose of this book is to offer a theoretical perspective and conceptual orientation to an element of physical education practice that has been increasingly recognised within the international physical education community as important. Rather than provide an instruction manual on assessment techniques in physical education, our focus is more broadly on the situation of assessment in the subject and the sociocultural influences on and consequences of assessment in physical education. We believe this perspective will be generative in terms of promoting further and broader research into physical education practices at various levels (systemic, institutional, interpersonal) and promoting practices within the field that optimise the contribution of assessment to physical education and constrain the unhelpful consequences of assessment. This sociocultural orientation recognises that the operations and effects of power and control in relation to assessment in physical education are necessary for optimising what Hayes *et al.* (2006) have described as 'productive assessment'. We recognise that assessment is a central feature of wider contemporary education practices and also has the potential for productive outcomes for learning within the subject and indeed for the subject itself. To understand assessment and support the realisation of its potential in physical education we must give due attention to the sociocultural factors associated with the practice.

Reflective of this intention to better understand the place and effect of assessment on physical education, we hope that this book makes a substantial contribution to discussion and debate regarding physical education assessment. While we will be proposing principles of assessment practice reflecting our view of the importance of the integration of assessment with curriculum and pedagogy and the pursuit of assessment efficacy, we do not claim that the principles are definitive (although we argue that they are defensible). Rather, we view our contribution as a participation in what we desire to be a generative dialogue within the international physical education community, focusing on more strategic and thoughtful utilisations of a process that is prominent in general education, is generally required in physical education, but as yet has not been given sufficient theoretical, conceptual or empirical attention in the field. The dialogue we are seeking to promote should address the problematic consequences of assessment in physical education as well as strategies for what Stobart described as 'the kinds of assessment that may improve the quality of learning' (2008, p. 171). Such a focus provides a platform to consider the potential contributions that assessment can make to the desired outcomes of physical education, including the unique and enduring learnings we hope all children and young people can experience.

As we highlighted at the beginning of this chapter, assessment operates as a 'message system' that communicates and ascribes meaning and value in physical education. The operation and outcomes of this message system thus serve as the fundamental orienting features of this book. The multiple levels at which value is communicated, as well as the interconnectedness of these levels, draws attention to the nature and ways in which assessment policies and practices in physical education frame understandings and experiences, from teacher and student perspectives. With this in view, Bernstein's theory of the pedagogic device (1996, 2000) provides a very helpful orienting framework and language to unpack the generation, transmission and effects of assessment messages in physical education. The book has been divided into three parts to focus particularly on practices within the different levels or fields of operation. Following this introductory chapter, the first part of the book sets a theoretical foundation for considerations of the place and outcomes of assessment across the education system. We then consider systemic influences such as the socio-political and education discourses and issues of physical education's status on the assessment message system in physical education. This includes the way in which assessment legitimises and promotes the acquisition, use and demon-stration of certain knowledges over others and encourages particular forms of 'pedagogical work' (Tinning, 2009) in physical education. Part I will thus establish the theoretical grounding and key conceptual reference points for the parts that follow.

The second part of the book focuses on the recontextualisation of the assessment message at the site of the school and physical education class and the reproduction of knowledge that results from the practices and pedagogical relations within physical education. Analysis and discussion will draw on Bourdieu's concepts of field, habitus and capital (e.g. 1986, 1989, 1990) to unpack the assessment process and its consequences for students, teachers, schools and physical education more broadly. Furthermore, this second part of the book will offer some arguably long-overdue theorising of validity in phy-sical education assessment. In particular we will draw on a sociocultural per-spective to consider the relationship between the consequences of assessment and its validity, and the promotion of a socially just physical education. Finally, in this section we will propose and discuss the idea of *assessment lit-eracy* as a way of conceptualising some of the broad learning consequences of assessment for physical education students. The section will also examine the critical linkages between assessment, ability, equity and inclusion. Part II will thus point to historical and ongoing challenges for policymakers, teachers and teacher educators in relation to assessment in physical education, and estab-lish key principles for intervening on the problematic practices and outcomes of assessment and promoting the productive effects of assessment for students in physical education.

Part III will build directly upon Parts I and II and explicitly engage with issues and challenges raised in preceding chapters. The focus in this part of the text is on future developments in, and the pedagogical potential of, assessment in physical education. The opening chapter in this section will address an impor-tant theme emerging from Parts I and II: the interlinkages and alignment of curriculum, pedagogy and assessment in physical education. This chapter will emphasise the need and potential for assessment to be recognised as a catalyst for pedagogical change in physical education directed towards greater equity. Significantly, we return to and expand on a set of assessment conditions that we have previously proposed (Hay and Penney, 2009) to support the realisation of *assessment efficacy*. The following chapter introduces 'contemporary relevance' and 'lifelong' and 'lifewide' learning as productive reference points in rethinking and reshaping assessment practices in physical education. The penultimate chapter in this section will centre on case studies in which contemporary developments in assessment will be presented and critiqued, and attention drawn to the role that new technologies may have in supporting assessment practices that are efficacious. Discussion draws directly on recent research and provide examples of ways in which some of the key challenges highlighted for physical education, and the field of human movement more generally, can be productively engaged with by education systems, institutions, schools and teachers. Finally, we conclude this book with an invitation to the international physical education community to engage in further discussion and debate regarding the issues raised and principles proposed in the book. Furthermore, we suggest future research possibilities and necessities for physical education assessment that we believe will provide more information on the role and impact of assessment as a message system in physical education and the conditions necessary for its optimal use and effect in the subject.

In the next chapter we present a summary of Basil Bernstein's theory of the pedagogic device, with a particular focus on the place of assessment within the device. Significantly, the pedagogic device provides both an explanatory language for the transmission and regulation of pedagogic discourse, consciousness and practice within education systems (including from the macro level through to the sites of engagement), as well as a set of reference points for considering the production, recontextualisation and reproduction of pedagogic discourse. The subsequent parts of this book draw quite deliberately on these reference points, particularly the recontextualising and secondary fields of the device.

Part I

Developing assessment 'messages' in physical education

2 Producing assessment messages

Introduction

In Chapter 1 we identified assessment as 'arguably one of the most influential facets of contemporary education' (p. 1) and established it as a social process and social activity. From this perspective, assessment always needs to be understood as socially, culturally, historically and politically situated and as being in a dynamic relation with the educational and social contexts in which it is set. Assessment is thus acknowledged as actively shaping education and social systems, as well as being shaped by them. With this in mind, we also established that our stance in relation to assessment and its educational and social potential is active rather than passive. Indeed, much of our motivation for this text lies in the scope that we see for assessment to be a means via which to make a positive difference to physical education, particularly from an equity perspective.

In introducing assessment as 'a message system' we highlighted that it is inherently linked to, and actively contributes to, the selection, classification and transmission of knowledge. Assessment within and beyond physical education is thus understood as communicating value and labelling and signalling particular skills, knowledge and understandings as being of more or less worth in contemporary education and wider society. It therefore also needs to be acknowledged as playing a part in creating and reaffirming social divisions and inequities. And while we identify assessment as a process that is characterised by complexity and negotiation and that, consequently, offers a space and means for action that is directed towards greater equity, we also stress that it is a process in which we are not all equally positioned or influential. Part of our exploration of assessment as a message system is, therefore, concerned with better understanding both the opportunities and limits that teachers in particular face in relation to prospective developments in assessment in physical education. It is also designed to extend critical engagement with assessment in relation to the range of knowledges that are recognised and promoted as having worth. Our focus in this chapter and Chapter 3 is, therefore, on 'the nature and consequences of particular systemic messages for schools, subjects, teachers and students' (Chapter 1, p. 5) and, critically, how particular messages are generated, legitimated and, potentially, challenged in physical education. We therefore explore the production, limits and control of assessment discourses in physical education, examining both content and process, and drawing insight and inspiration from the work of Bernstein (1990, 1996, 2000) in particular. In response to the possible reaction, 'why Bernstein?', we share Moore's (2011) view that arguably one of the most significant features of Bernstein's work is 'its power to generate so much energy in thinking and research across the world' (p. xv). As Moore (2011, p. xv) articulated, Bernstein's legacy lies in the fact that his work 'provides so many places *within which* to work, but, also, so many tools *with which* to work. Bernstein's theory "works" because it can be *put to work* by so many others.' For us it is also vital that any such endeavours are in tune with Bernstein's underlying desire, to open up debate about matters within and beyond education as they relate to social inequality and justice and, in so doing, also to extend that debate to prospective 'better futures' for physical education and society. As Bernstein (2000, p. xix) explained:

> Education can have a crucial role in creating tomorrow's optimism in the context of today's pessimism. But if it is to do this then we must have an analysis of social biases in education. These biases lie deep within the very structure of the education system's process of transmission and acquisition and their social assumptions.

Introducing the pedagogic device as a tool for analysis of assessment in physical education

In introducing his 2000 text Bernstein expressed uncertainty about re-presenting a chapter focusing on the pedagogic device, pointing out that much of the work presented could be found in his 1990 work, *Class, codes and control* (Vol. IV). In developing the work presented here, we have found it useful to refer to Bernstein's various commentaries and reflections (Bernstein 1990, 1996, 2000) centring on 'the pedagogic device' as a *regulator* of pedagogic discourse, consciousness and practice but also, simultaneously, the key to the generation of communication and practice that ultimately *challenges that regulation*. Introducing the device, Bernstein (2000) explained that, by its own internal rules, the pedagogic device 'regulates fundamentally the communication it makes possible' and, thereby, 'acts selectively on meaning potential'; that is, 'the potential discourse that is available to be pedagogised' (p. 27). Our interest in the pedagogic device thus relates directly to limits to and control of meaning in the contexts of physical education (and, more particularly, assessment in physical education) in and through the production, recontextualisation and transmission of discourses. Following Bernstein, we emphasise that these processes and, thus, the rules of and associated with the pedagogic device are not ideologically neutral. The pedagogic device is a crucial site of symbolic control (Bernstein 1990, 1996, 2000). Bernstein's work provides concepts and analytical tools via which the better to engage with this control as it relates to historical and contemporary thinking and practices in assessment in physical education and, also, contemporary education systems and structures. The latter emphasis reflects our concern to consider structural and symbolic influences on thinking about assessment in physical education, and the dynamic between them. The pedagogic device facilitates such analysis.

The pedagogic device has a dual focus and two related dimensions. It simultaneously encompasses the means and mechanisms of 'relay' (of meaning and discourse) and 'what is relayed' (particular meanings and discourses). Bernstein identified that the device is constituted by relatively stable, internal rules, while the communication arising from the device is 'contextually regulated' (Bernstein, 2000, p. 27). His emphasis was, therefore, that the 'forms of realisation of the pedagogic device ... are subject to rules *which vary with the context*' (p. 27, our emphasis), with the variation in forms of realisation serving to 'restrict or enhance the potential discourse available to be pedagogised' (p. 28) *in any given context*. The 'potential range of communicative outcomes' (p. 27) made possible by the pedagogic device similarly then need to be acknowledged as context specific. *Contextual specificity*, in relation to rules, potential discourses and their pedagogic expression, is of interest to us as, in essence, variations in context directly impact upon the potential to extend possibilities for thought and meaning in ways that can challenge the 'rules and classifying systems' internal to the pedagogic device. In the sections that follow we therefore endeavour to explore the pedagogic device as we see it relating to assessment in physical education. Here and in subsequent chapters our interest is particularly in the generation and regulation of contextual rules for pedagogic communication, specific to 'physical education' and/or 'assessment', and the ways in which these may serve to reaffirm or mediate inherently more stable internal rules of the pedagogic device.

At this point it is appropriate to draw attention to a crucial caveat in what can potentially appear to be an analysis firmly focused on limits and constraints. Bernstein was always very clear in his emphasis that the pedagogic device 'is not deterministic in its consequences' (ibid., p. 38). He explained that 'it is possible to have an outcome, a form of communication *which can subvert the fundamental rules of the device*' (p. 28, our emphasis). The pedagogic device, as articulated by Bernstein, thus prompts us to question and further explore the discourses that are 'available to be pedagogised' in contexts of physical education, assessment and, specifically, assessment in physical education, with an interest in both constraint and possibility. In the discussion that follows we therefore examine the rules internal to the device and regulating the pedagogic communication arising from it in these particular contexts, with a view to not merely better understanding sustained characteristics of assessment practices in physical education but, also, ways in which opportunities for alternative thinking and practices can be recognised and pursued.

Boundaries and classifications

Before directing attention specifically towards rules that constitute the peda-gogic device, we take a step back and acknowledge another central feature of Bernstein's thinking and theorising: the notion of 'boundary'. 'Boundary' is a key metaphor in Bernstein's work (Bernstein, 2000). It is fundamental to his articulation of curriculum and pedagogical divisions and distinctions, and their social significance in terms of symbolic control. Yet, simultaneously, Bernstein used 'boundary' to reveal the prospect of countering this control, drawing attention to permeability and possibility. His emphasis was that:

> The crucial metaphorising is *what the boundary signifies.* Condensing the past but not a relay for it, rather a tension between the past and possible futures. The boundary is not etched as in copperplate nor as ephemeral as in quicksand, and is sometimes more enabling than disabling.
>
> (Bernstein, 2000, xiii, original emphasis)

Bernstein's concern with boundaries encompassed power-, knowledge- and pedagogic relations, and the various policy and pedagogic processes that therefore both construct and relay boundaries, 'so as to distribute, shape, position and opposition forms of consciousness' (ibid., p. xiii). In this regard, it is notable that he posed this question of the pedagogic device: 'are the rules and classifying systems built into the device in some way regulating what comes out of it?' (ibid., p. 27). Talk of 'classifying systems' draws our attention to boundaries inherent in the structuring of knowledge, communication and pedagogy that are internal to the device and, as such, might appear impene-trable. Yet, simultaneously, recognising that any system of classification gen-erates its own tensions reminds us that the device can never completely regulate its own consequences:

> Although the device is there to control the thinkable, in the process of controlling the unthinkable it makes the possibility of the unthinkable available. Therefore, internal to the device is its own paradox: it cannot control that which it has been set up to control.
>
> (Bernstein, 2000, p. 38)

Our discussion here reflects that we regard boundaries and systems of classi-fication as valuable foci via which to pursue this paradox. We are also very aware that Bernstein's language can be dense and that it is not always easy to see meaningful application or significance of his concepts or statements. So, what are some of the boundaries that we see as significant (and, in important respects, 'defining') in relation to how teachers, students, other education professionals and policymakers all think about assessment in physical education? Throughout this text we consider assessment as it relates to curriculum and pedagogy. In many instances we problematise distinctions (certainly rigid ones) and direct attention to relations between curriculum, pedagogy and assessment. This latter emphasis highlights the possibilities for thinking differently that just engaging with boundaries can open up. As soon as we consider a boundary we are prompted to think not only of the distinctions that it signals, but also the relations that it both reflects and enables us to explore and potentially enhance. Thus, if we return to our prime focus on assessment, it becomes important to question what, in any particular pedagogical context, defines or identifies assessment as such? If we think specifically about a physical education lesson, what would prompt either the students or an observer to recognise part of that lesson 'as assessment'? And, what would lead us or others to query whether a learning experience constitutes (legitimate) assessment? As we discuss further in the chapters that follow, how we conceive of assessment reflects the purposes we associate with it. Furthermore, it has implications for not only *what* skills, knowledge and understandings are considered legitimate and important for assessment in physical education to address but, also, the possibilities we will recognise and consider in relation to *how* to assess, *when* and *where* assessment might occur in physical education and *who* has what (legitimate) role in the process. Following Bernstein, therefore, we engage with boundaries from spatial, temporal and, particularly, relational perspectives and reaffirm that systemic boundaries always also have a symbolic meaning and function.

In Chapter 7 we explore Arnold's (1979) three dimensions of education 'about', 'through' and 'in' movement. These dimensions represent a system of classification and provide a framework for thinking about physical education in a way that generates its own particular order and structure. It is simultaneously enabling and constraining, as each dimension provides its own unique focus for learning and, prospectively, assessment, but in so doing, generates the risk that arguably the most important aspect of the framework – the inter-relatedness of the dimensions – is marginalised or lost. We prompt an enhanced focus on the dynamic between the three dimensions and reaffirm that, in order to do this effectively, we need to develop better linkages between curriculum, pedagogy and assessment in physical education.

Arnold's dimensions and other 'systems of classification' that we explore through this text relate to our underlying interest in equity in physical education. In several chapters we prompt critical reflection about the basis upon which particular students will be deemed 'able' and others 'less able' in physical education. What is it that defines such a line and, in so doing, labels and distinguishes students from one another, conveys a sense of worth to some students and denies this for others? Equally, what is it that means something will be deemed evidence of learning in physical education? What do teachers read into and from student performance and interactions in a lesson in this regard? As we have discussed previously (Hay and Penney, 2009; Penney and Hay, 2008), assessment and assessment judgements in physical education are underpinned by particular conceptualisations of ability and particular thinking about the skills, knowledge and understandings that 'physical education' encompasses or excludes.

This brief discussion has sought to convey the value of exploring various boundaries and systems of classification that are embedded in, and legitimated and conveyed by, assessment in physical education. The pedagogic device relates directly to these processes and provides conceptual direction for our efforts to gain a better grasp on them.

Rules and regulation

Above we pointed to systems of classification as generating not only particular meanings but, also, order and structure. The pedagogic device is fundamental to the production and regulation of order in meaning and consciousness, and the power-relations upon which the production and regulation rests. It is integral to and creative of the dynamic between power-relations and knowledge-relations, in that it comprises three sets of hierarchically related rules 'for specializing[1] forms of consciousness' (Bernstein, 1990, p. 181): *distributive*, *recontextualising* and *evaluative* rules. Bernstein (2000) explained that: 'the rules of the pedagogic device are essentially implicated in the distribution of, and constraints upon, the various forms of consciousness' (p. 28) such that 'whoever appropriates the device, appropriates a crucial site for symbolic control' (p. 38).

Distributive rules can be seen as simultaneously playing a creative and regulatory role in that they 'specialise forms of knowledge, forms of consciousness and forms of practice to social groups' (Bernstein, 2000, p. 28). They 'distribute forms of consciousness through distributing different forms of knowledge' (ibid., p. 28). Thus, distributive rules are the means via which specialist forms of knowledge come to be defined as such and, in parallel, they represent the means via which access to those specialist forms of knowledge is also defined, limited and regulated. They 'mark and distribute who may transmit what to whom and under what conditions, and they attempt to set the outer limits of legitimate discourse' (ibid., p. 31). They are, then, key to the *production* of discourse in terms of content and authority/control. Bernstein (2000) explained that: 'the distributive rules create a specialised field of production of discourses, with specialised rules of access and specialised controls' (p. 31). Key questions then arising are who and what exercises influence over that field?, with Bernstein's contention being that this field 'is controlled more and more by the state itself' (p. 31).

The notion of 'outer limit' (framed by distributive rules) is useful to keep in mind, given that the subsequent rules we discuss are derived from distributive rules. In this sense, the field of production of education discourse determines the forms of legitimate knowledge and associated discourses that are accessible and available (able to be thought) within specialised contexts such as physical education. The boundaries of the specialist context, in terms of the discourses available to be selectively appropriated and refocused to inform thinking in the field, are effectively drawn by distributive rules shaping the production of discourse. We can thus reflect that discourses of accountability, validity, reliability, educational pragmatism, equity and lifelong learning may all be amongst the discourses 'available' amidst a development focused on assessment in physical education. Yet we are equally aware that their relative positioning, and scope for expression and development, will vary with time and context, will not be neutral and are a function of the distributive rules.

Bernstein's analysis consistently prompts us to always consider regulation of knowledge from the perspective of 'who' and 'how' in conjunction with 'the what'. This interplay is central to the pedagogic device and is particularly evident in the rules and arenas we now turn attention to, concerned with *recontextualisation*.

The second set of rules integral to the pedagogic device Bernstein termed 'recontextualising rules', reflecting the derivative nature of the rules and conveying that discursive boundaries of/for the processes that we now focus on have been set by the production of discourse. The rules, and the fields that they create, relate to the *relocation* of discourse and, more specifically, the selective appropriation, refocusing and positioning of discourses amidst this relocation. Bernstein identified that recontextualising rules relate directly to the regulation of specific *pedagogic discourse*. As reflected in Bernstein's own commentary, terminology becomes complex and to some extent problematic here. In developing the concept of pedagogic discourse Bernstein (2000) referred to it *as* 'a recontextualising principle' (p. 33), but also explained it as itself *constructed by* that principle, 'which selectively appropriates, relocates, refocuses and relates other discourses to constitute its own order' (p. 33). Thus, he was then able to say that 'pedagogic discourse is generated by recontextualising discourse' (p. 33), arising in *recontextualising fields* and by *recontextualising agents*. While we always need to recall the boundaries set for recontextualising rules, fields and agents by the field of production of discourse, the recontextualising fields are nevertheless sites of notable contestation and negotiation of discourse and texts. As such, they are fundamental to 'creating, maintaining, changing, and legitimating discourse, transmission, and organizational practices which regulate the internal orderings of pedagogic discourse' (Bernstein, 1990, p. 193).

So, who is involved in the recontextualising fields and how does what occurs in and through these fields impact upon possibilities for assessment in physical education? If we focus first on the latter, the significance is well captured in this clarifying comment from Bernstein (2000, p. 34): 'the recontextualising principle not only recontexualises the *what* of pedagogic discourse, what discourse is to become subject and content of pedagogic practice. It also recontextualises the *how*; that is, *the theory of instruction*' (original emphasis); inherent in which is a particular conceptualisation of students, teachers and legitimate pedagogical relations. From this perspective, we can see that recontextualisation has a critical role to play in shaping what we recognise as appropriate, legitimate and possible *content and modes* of assessment in any specialised context. This is achieved through the creation of a relation between two discourses: *instructional discourse* (creating 'specialised skills and their relationship to each other') and *regulative discourse* ('a discourse of social order') (ibid., pp. 31–32). 'Pedagogic discourse is the rule which leads to the embedding of one discourse in another, to create one text, to create *one* discourse' (ibid., p. 32, original emphasis). Instructional discourse is embedded in regulative discourse, such that the dominance of regulative discourse is established and its function is to generate the 'internal order' of instructional discourse. This reflects that pedagogic discourse '*is a recontextualising principle*' (ibid., p. 33). It acts to brings together, 'as one', 'the what' – 'the categories, contents, and relationships to be transmitted, that is their *classification*' – and 'the how' – 'the manner of their transmission' or *framing* (Bernstein, 1990, p. 196, original emphasis). Throughout this text we emphasise the fundamental dynamic between classification and framing, and its importance in considering the regulation of assessment in physical education and endeavours to explore the limits of that regulation.

Keeping our focus on *pedagogic discourse*, we now turn to two recontextualising fields identified by Bernstein: an 'official recontextualising field' (ORF) and a 'pedagogic recontextualising field' (PRF). Both fields involve agents in the movement and (regulated) transformation of texts. In exploring them our prime interest is in the scope that recontextualising rules provide for the meanings that texts contain and convey to be contested and mediated in either field, and *by whom*. These are, then, sites of struggle 'over and amidst' the construction of pedagogic discourse.

The ORF, PRF and assessment in physical education

Bernstein identified the ORF as 'created and dominated by the state and its selected agents and ministries' (2000, p. 33), operating in national and local government arenas. The ORF thus encompasses official education structures, their inherent legislative and administrative systems and relations, and the individuals that the systems define as legitimate agents in the field. It functions to create, maintain and change 'official pedagogic discourse' (Bernstein, 1990). Bernstein's own commentaries and an extensive body of research and literature focused on contemporary education policy have pointed to the growing complexity of this field and its mechanisms of control. Variously, studies in education policy sociology have revealed the ways in which increasingly enhanced regulation of the content and form of education has been achieved and is being maintained through *the combined effects* of multiple policies *and* the conditions (and power-relations) they have served to create (see for example Macdonald, 2011; Penney and Evans, 2005). The extent of impact of any particular policy development has essentially rested in parallel developments and what we might term 'collective policy impact'.

From this perspective, we emphasise that it is invariably meaningless to consider the prospective influence of curriculum developments or 'reforms' without looking simultaneously at the regulations and requirements that accompany them relating to assessment, reporting, institutional funding and teacher education. Furthermore, we highlight that, increasingly, the *breadth and scope* of education policy initiatives are a key means via which both 'the what' and 'the how' of pedagogic discourse are being regulated. In 1998 Ball identified the contemporary global context as one in which 'new forms of state steering and regulation' (p. 120) have emerged and whereby the 'rules of engagement' (ibid.) in policy arenas have been both rewritten and reframed amidst changed (but not entirely deconstructed) policy structures and relations. This captures the capacity of the ORF to 'self regulate' amidst its own change, and Bernstein's (1990) observation that new relations within the field could be associated with (and are designed for) new regulatory potential. Following Bernstein (1990), we recognise that, if we consider the case of physical education, 'there may be more than one Ministry active in this recontextualizing field' (p. 196). This is a contemporary reality that many readers will relate to. It is clearly evidenced and made explicit in the discourse of Physical Education and School Sport (PESS) in the UK and commentaries internationally (see, for example, Fry and McNeil, 2011; Petrie and lisahunter, 2011). Bernstein (1990) also identified that the ORF 'may incorporate, selectively, specialized services from agents/agencies external to it, which in turn alter the position of these agents in their respective fields' (p. 196). In education and physical education specifically, there are numerous instances of agents and agencies from other industry sectors and from overseas being called upon to inform policy development. Governments internationally will selectively look to, and invite input from 'external experts'. Consequences that we see arising in relation to assessment are a narrowing of official pedagogic discourse internationally and the embedding and increasing dominance of discourses of accountability and performativity in assessment discourses.

Drawing insight from Ball (1990) we suggest that inviting agents and agencies external to a specialised field to provide services and input to it directly impacts relations and relative 'authority to speak' within the field. It thus reshapes the ORF in terms of individuals' relative capacity to contest and influence pedagogic discourse. Policy analyses such as that undertaken by Evans and Penney (1995) and Glover (2001) have vividly revealed the 'politics of selection' at play in physical education curriculum development and the constant dynamic between 'the who' and 'how' of policy (Gale, 2003) within and beyond the ORF. We see clear scope and a need for more research that draws on education policy sociology and centres specifically on the development of new statutory assessment frameworks for physical education in primary, secondary and senior secondary phases of schooling. Further, we suggest that a key issue that such research needs to engage with is the relation between the ORF and PRF and, thus, the role the PRF can play in countering the dominance of discourses repeatedly privileged in official texts.

Bernstein (1990) observed that: 'We can define the relative autonomy of pedagogic discourse to the extent that the pedagogic recontextualizing fields (PRF) are permitted to exist and affect official pedagogic practice' (p. 198). It is arguably this relative autonomy that many actors within the PRF would acknowledge has been progressively eroded in recent years. Bernstein identified the PRF as comprising universities, departments and colleges of education, private research foundations, specialist education media and their publications and publishing houses and noted that the PRF 'may extend to fields not specialized in educational discourse and its practices, but which are able to exert influence both on the State and its various arrangements and/or upon special sites, agents and practices within education' (Bernstein, 1990, p. 192). The structural characteristics and relations within the PRF, and between agents/agencies within it and those within the ORF, are significant in considering the PRF's prospective 'movement and transformation of texts'. As Bernstein (1990) recognised, the PRF can be 'strongly classified internally, producing sub-fields specialized to levels of the education system, curricula, groups of pupils' (p. 198). Thus, we can conceive of senior secondary physical education, secondary physical education and primary physical education as sub-fields and reflect upon what the extent of the insulation between them means for the appropriation, relocation and refocusing of discourses within them. We specifically question the breadth of discourses that will feature in any sub-field amidst strong classification, and the consequential prospects for establishing new thinking about assessment in physical education at any of these levels. Similarly, the relative insulation of physical education from other subject-based sub-fields of education is apparent. In some instances, this may be seen as enabling contestation and negotiation of discourse, debate and thinking about assessment, that may be constrained amidst weaker classification. From this perspective, the strong insulation of the sub-field can be seen as, to some extent, providing physical educationalists with the space to generate interpretations of discourse and text that would not otherwise be possible. But, equally, we see limitations inherent in the insulation, recognising that weaker classification may generate engagement with other discourses (located in/with other sub-fields) and, in so doing, could also extend the capacity of the specialised sub-field to effectively contest pedagogic discourse and its practices. This latter stance was reflected to some extent in Penney's (2008) call for physical education to strategically appropriate a number of discourses including lifelong learning and personalised learning that, at the time, clearly held political appeal within and beyond the UK. It also remains, however, a stance that we acknowledge needs to be pursued with caution, and particularly if we are concerned with assessment in physical education.

Opinions will differ about the extent to which individuals within the PRF are likely to be able to simultaneously 'engage with and resist' some of the dominant contemporary discourses in and of assessment and, thus, whether they should actively engage with particular discourses. Yet, as Penney (2008) eluded, the question that we are faced with may well be whether we can afford *not to engage* with particular discourses. The removal of (or certainly open reduction in) the capacity of individuals within the PRF to make such choices reflects a critical shift in policy and discursive relations. As we indicated above, in many countries the state can be seen as having tightened control over the ORF and, furthermore, as acting to reduce the autonomy of the PRF. The outcome is reduced capacity for struggle over pedagogic discourse. We now turn attention to the implications of this trend by considering the third set of rules integral to the pedagogic device, which are derived from recontextualising rules (and thus, pedagogic discourse): *evaluative rules.*

From pedagogic discourse to pedagogic practice: evaluative rules

Evaluative rules relate directly to pedagogic practice 'as cultural relay' (Bernstein, 1990, p. 65). Inherent in this is the notion of pedagogic practice 'as a social form and as a specific content' (ibid., p. 63). They relate to the (regulated) transformation of pedagogic discourse to pedagogic practice. Once again Bernstein's conceptualisation encompasses a dynamic, in this instance between rules that constitute 'the "how" of any practice' and, then, the ways in which the 'particular "how" created by any set of rules acts selectively on the "what" of the practice, the form of its content' (p. 63). Pedagogic relations are thus central to the relay, with Bernstein identifying that 'the essential logic of any pedagogic relation consists of the relationship essentially between three rules' (ibid., p. 65): *hierarchical, sequencing* and *criterial*, with hierarchical dominant. Hierarchical rules relate to the power-relations associated with being a transmitter or acquirer in the pedagogic relation and the space that these provide for negotiation within those roles. Sequencing rules reflect that progression is a necessary feature of any pedagogic practice, and sequencing rules will also, inherently, address *pacing*: the rate of expected learning in relation to the pattern of progression defined by the sequencing rules. Criterial rules enable recognition and understanding of 'what counts as legitimate or illegitimate communication, social relation, or position' (ibid., p. 66).

Individually and collectively, these rules provide us with a critical lens for reflection on established and prospective alternative assessment practices in physical education, in different phases of education and various learning contexts. Bernstein again provides us with tools to question 'the logic' of pedagogic practice that invariably goes unquestioned. In this instance, it relates to the particular skills, knowledge and understandings that are assessed in physical education, at any particular time, in particular contexts and by particular means. We can apply this thinking to, for example, a complete year's programme of physical education, any unit of work within it, or any particular lesson. The questioning remains pertinent. What content are we privileging in and through the assessment tasks, contexts and modes used? What anticipated progression and pace is implicit or explicit in our assessment plans and design? What communication of learning are we enabling or denying in assessment?

Taken together, the rules, and questions they give rise to, lead us to then ask how inclusive of all students' learning needs and interests current assessment practices are. At the same time, we anticipate that the sorts of questions we have posed will generate responses that point to an awareness that multiple factors shape thinking about what constitute possible, legitimate, feasible and/or valid assessment practices in physical education in any given context. Some will be factors specific to physical education or specific learning contexts or activities associated with it. Official curriculum or syllabus specifications, and expectations (formalised or not) for particular phases of education or year groups will also come into play. Thinking and decisions about assessment in physical education will also reflect broader social and political contexts within which teachers are working and schools are operating.

While we are clearly reminded that evaluative rules need to be viewed in hierarchical relation to distributive and recontextualisation rules, and that opportunities to deviate from established assessment practice may often seem limited, there is nevertheless a need to recall that some 'scope for slippage' (Bowe *et al.*, 1992; Penney and Evans, 1999) always remains amidst any individual instance of the transformation of texts and discourses to pedagogic practice of assessment in physical education. As we emphasised earlier, the pedagogic device is not a deterministic framework. Arguably, it is in the arena of 'assessment as pedagogy' (see also Chapters 7, 8 and 9) that there may be the greatest potential for the boundaries of thinking about assessment in physical education to be extended in ways that serve to enhance equity.

Assessment messages and the potential outputs of the pedagogic device

In this final section of the chapter, we turn attention to the outputs that Bernstein (1990) outlined as prospectively arising from the pedagogic device. He suggested that there were two possible and oppositional outputs: 'either shared competences or graded specialist performances (and sometimes combinations with different emphases)' (p. 206). The respective orientation of these two outputs differs from an educational and social standpoint. Bernstein associates them as arising from two different types of 'pedagogic agency'. He explained that creation of shared competences is intrinsic to an agency that:

> is not designed to facilitate individual differences; rather it is designed to ensure that all have the same range of competences/practices. It is not designed to promote explicitly, as part of its rules, specialized performances. This is not to say that some individuals will not, in fact, be more effective in performances based upon these shared competences, only that the pedagogic agency is not explicitly designed to bring it about.
>
> (Ibid., p. 207)

The social relations created from this agency are 'similar to' relations. In comparison, those arising from agency oriented to specialist performances are 'different from' relations (Bernstein, 1990). The agenda is very clearly different. 'Such a pedagogic agency is concerned to bring about specialized differences between individuals: differences in their performances. Such an output points to gradings, not only within but also between specialisms' (p. 207).

The differences in pedagogic agency as described by Bernstein prompt us to reflect on assessment in physical education from social, systemic and pedagogic perspectives and ponder what scope there is in contemporary physical education to counter the dominant focus on 'different from'. The different outputs both reflect and are at the same time a relay for contrasting societies and values. Bernstein identified that 'the potential outputs of the device seem to be relays for weak or strong classification based upon work, weak or strong emphasis upon technological development, low or high levels of differentiated consumption' (p. 208). It is also interesting to note that, writing in 1990, he considered that possibly 'as the complexity of the social division of labour weakens, as a consequence of the "communication revolution" ... then there may well be an enlargement of the pedagogic space which could relay shared competences' (p. 208).

We are aware that, in some respects, commentary such as this can appear remote from the 'here and now' practical reality of assessment in physical education. Yet, at the same time we challenge those perceptions of remoteness and come back to individual agency as always present and always influential in and amidst 'the bigger picture' of educational, social and cultural relay. All pedagogic practice and, thus, any act of assessment, is integral to that relay, and as such can have a reproductive or transformative focus. In this sense evaluative rules are enabling, not merely constraining.

Concluding comments

This chapter has centred on conceptualisations of educational and social processes that are undoubtedly challenging to engage with. We acknowledge the complexity of Bernstein's work and make no claims to have offered a flawless or complete commentary. Rather, we hope that we have captured some of the rich potential for his work to inform critical inquiry focused on assessment in physical education. This text reflects our view that assessment in physical education is currently calling out for more attention, conceptually and empirically. The pedagogic device encourages and facilitates highly focused analysis and deep thought. We hope that this chapter, like the device, can be generative.

In the next chapter we focus our attention on the activity and effects of assessment as it operates as a message system to communicate and confer value in the curriculum and on individuals and groups within the system itself. As we have argued in this chapter, Bernstein's concepts, which we continue to utilise in understanding the assessment message system, draw critical focus on the practices and outcomes of educational technologies such as assessment as well as helping us to identify and understand the contexts and conditions of practice that may be considered as 'enabling'.

3 Definitions, differentiations and communications of assessment

Introduction

It is helpful to consider why certain aspects of school curricula appear to be more important than other areas and to ascertain the features of the education system that inform these apparent differentiations. If we accept the proposal that schools and school curricula are socially constructed phenomena (e.g. Goodson, 1997), we will be comfortable with the idea that differences in the value of subjects and subject matter are not inherent, but rather outcomes of the curriculum contestations of stakeholders whose value-laden contributions are informed by particular principled positions regarding the formation of the ideal citizen (Hunter, 1994). The value-laden distinctions between certain elements of the general curriculum and within a specific subject curriculum that arise from this contestation need to be communicated to the system in order for their realisation across the system. However, it is clear that the system supports other forms of value-based differentiations. Consider, for example, the distinctions that are made between high-achieving schools and low-achieving schools in the generation of school league tables, and between students in senior secondary contexts for the purposes of selection into post-schooling avenues. Assessment is an important site and mechanism for the generation, communication and application of these valued differentiations. Failing to recognise that assessment, intentionally or otherwise, is a communicative technology can render one reasonably ambivalent to the contribution that it makes to the transfer of these values, and the content and effects of the discourses that assessment specifically communicates. With this in mind, in this chapter we build on the theoretical foundations provided in Chapter 2 to discuss how assessment operates as a communication system. To do so, we continue to draw on the work of Basil Bernstein and elaborate on his notion of the message systems of education.

Bernstein proposed that the selection, classification, transmission and assessment of educational knowledge could be viewed as occurring through the three inter-related message systems of pedagogy, curriculum and evaluation (Bernstein, 1971). The use of the term 'message system' is significant as it draws attention to what is being communicated, as well as the means of communicating the message. The message systems of curriculum and pedagogy are generally the ones most broadly understood and that are most operationally obvious. At a simple level, the curriculum message system operates in the education system to define *what* should be taught and learnt (the content of the message) and is most often communicated in texts such as syllabus documents and text books (the means of communication) as well as more tacitly through the 'hidden curriculum'. The pedagogy message system specifies a relationship between the deliverer (teacher) and acquirer (student) of knowledge and brings to the fore the *processes or techniques* through which the delivery and/or acquisition of content and discourse might occur. Assessment as a message system essentially operates to define, communicate and ascribe *value*, and to ascertain the extent to which educational practices and outcomes are aligned with expectations (be they curricular or pedagogical). The intention to assess a particular educational element (such as certain knowledge and practical skills, or performance attributes) conveys the expectation that these elements are of sufficient interest to particular stakeholders to warrant attention. Irrespective of whether we are considering an education system, or teacher and student interaction, some facets of a learning field are assessed and others are not, and by implication a distinction is made between the relative values of those facets. Similarly, assessment provides a mechanism for assigning value (e.g. in the form of grades in institutional academic settings) to those who demonstrate the possession of valued knowledge and skills in a valued manner.

While individually the three message systems have an internal logic and function to them, it is the *inter*dependence of the three systems that has the most impact on the communication of discourses within institutional education settings. In this regard it is helpful to consider the systems as interconnected cogs where the adjustment of practice/content/expectation in one system affects these elements in the other two systems. Of course, the three message systems are themselves affected by the education systems in which they are located so that 'issues of pedagogies, social justice and inclusion cannot be considered in isolation from those of curricula and assessment' (Lingard and Mills, 2007, p. 235) or the possibilities they frame for subjects, teachers and students. While observing this relationship, several education commentators have noted the *peculiar* effect of assessment on the other two message systems (e.g. Darling-Hammond, 2010; Lingard, 2010; Stobart, 2008). Lingard (2010) has observed, for example, that 'the evaluation system (manifest as high-stakes national census testing) has taken the upper hand in many schooling systems around the world' (p. 131), implying not only its prominence in the thinking and practices of schools, teachers and students, but also its marked effect on the curricular and pedagogical practices in the classroom.

There are numerous examples of the effect of assessment on the curricula and pedagogical possibilities within education systems internationally. Arguably the most compelling examples of this come from the state-based schooling systems of the USA, where testing (a notably narrow form of assessment) has been the main driver of educational practice, propagating a text-book driven curriculum tightly wed to the foci of systematic tests (McNeil, 2000) and affecting the offering of a physical education in many of the systems. The curriculum and pedagogic impact of 'SATs' (Statutory Assessment Tests) in England and Wales similarly stands out as illustrating the dominance and wide-reaching influence of discourses of accountability and performativity in contemporary education policy and practice. Shifting focus to the Southern Hemisphere, we again note in Australia the impact of the National Assessment Program – Literacy and Numeracy (NAPLAN) and the associated My School website (which publically communicates the outcomes of NAPLAN for every Australian school) on curriculum and pedagogical expectations at a systemic level and at the level of individual schools. In this instance the 'stakes' of the tests, which are sat by every Year 3, 5, 7 and 9 student in the country, have been raised by tying teacher and principal performance to the school's NAPLAN result and by reporting this data on the publically accessible My School website. The My School website lists a school's result against national averages and also its performance against 60 socio-economically similar schools across the country. The consequences of this national agenda have included test-focused rationalisations of general and school curricula with additional curricular priority given to literacy and numeracy at the expense of other elements of the curriculum (Lingard, 2010), including (health) and physical education. Similarly, Lingard noted that NAPLAN was having a narrowing effect on the pedagogies of schools where student-oriented pedagogies were being replaced by more teacher-centred and didactic approaches, 'with this having its most egregious effects in low SES [socio-economic status] schools' (2010, p. 131).

The consistency of the role of assessment in education systems internationally is attributable in many ways to the globalisation of education, which itself is underpinned and driven by systemic comparative measures such as the Programme for International Student Assessment (PISA), Trends in International Mathematics and Science Study (TIMSS) and the Progress in International Reading Literacy Study (PIRLS). While the organisations that develop these measures, including the OECD and the International Association for the Evaluation of Educational Achievement (IEA), view these measures as indicators of system quality and equity, they have become significant drivers of institutional reform and definers of curriculum value at international and national levels (Rizvi and Lingard, 2010). The globalising effects on education of these international measures and their impact on curriculum representation at a national level has implications for the place and constitution of physical education as a subject, as well as the practices of assessment within it. It raises questions regarding what might be viewed as the educational merits of the subject as well as how to respond as a subject community to such a powerful reforming force. Should the field present itself in terms that resonate with the valued discourses communicated by these international measures, or should it make a more concerted communication of the unique learning and contribution that physical education can make to the educational experiences and life futures of students? These are significant matters for the field to grapple with and highlight the fact that discussions regarding assessment in physical education need to move beyond just the techniques or tools of assessment and more overtly encompass the role and impact of assessment as a message system on the purpose and practice of the subject itself.

The role of assessment as a communicator of value is well established in general educational literature. In contrast, this work of assessment has not been equally investigated or understood in the field of physical education, even though the valuing work of assessment at an institutional level has arguably affected the status of the subject in this arena. These values can be explicit or implicit in their transmission and are evident at both the macro and micro levels of the education system. It is important that we recognise that the macro and micro contexts are interdependent and that the valuing work of assessment at one level inevitably affects the practices and consequences of the other. Nevertheless, for the purpose of drawing specific attention to aspects of the valuing work of the assessment message system we will be considering the macro contexts and micro contexts separately. We now turn our attention to consideration of the effects of assessment as a communicator of value at a systemic or macro level, including the impact of assessment on the administration of education systems, and the constitution and value of school curriculum elements.

Assessment value at the macro level

Accountability is a primary function of assessment at the systemic level and it operates both to communicate the valued facets of curriculum and education policy and to determine the extent to which these values are being manifest in the practices of schools and teachers, and in the defined performances of students. These roles are significant features of contemporary neoliberal approaches to education administration in many Western systems that are themselves characterised by discourses such as rights to individual choice and consumerism (Ranson, 2003). Ball (2003) suggested that the education reform agenda of the neoliberal society is 'embedded in three interrelated policy technologies; the market, managerialism, and performativity' (p. 215). Ball (2003) explained that these three technologies play an important role in the new management of public resources, in which the former bureaucracies are aligned with the methods, culture and ethical system of the private sector. According to Meadmore and Meadmore (2004) performativity refers to 'a technology, a culture, and a mode of regulation, that employs judgement, comparisons, and displays as means of control, attrition, and change' (p. 376). Within the context of schools and education systems particular forms of assessment are central to the technology of performativity (Broadfoot, 1998;

Lingard and Blackmore, 1997), for it is through the processes of systemic and standardised assessment measures, and the meritocratic assumptions that underpin them, that a currency of performativity can be generated. This particular currency is the student performance data, the levels or qualifiers of which are used to 'mark' or identify programmes and institutions of quality. This approach places significant demands on the work of teachers (Smyth *et al.*, 2000) as their own performance is dependent upon the success of their students within this performative culture. We will say more on this later.

It is noteworthy that in many Western education systems schools are commonly using student performance data to represent themselves in an education marketplace (Kenway and Bullen, 2001), typified for example in the context of Queensland secondary schools by the advertising of the number of 'OP1s'[1] that students at the school achieved on their street-side school notice boards and the prominence of positive school performance data on school websites. Such market approaches have been encouraged by significant political figures and through the media as a supposed means of optimising education quality through competitive market principles. This market-oriented or corporatised schooling is a complex ideological construction as it draws on notions of democracy, yet fails to articulate the purpose of schooling in relation to this choice. In relation to the greater choice supposedly offered by this approach to administrating schooling, Bernstein (1990) explained that the

> explicit commitment to greater choice by parents and pupils is not a celebration of participatory democracy but a thin cover for the old stratification of schools and curricula. New forms of assessment, profiling, criteria-referenced rather than norm-referenced assessment, allegedly to recognize and liberate individual qualities, allow of, and mark, greater control of assessment.
>
> (p. 87)

The market approach as the organising and motivating feature of schooling has been central to educational reforms in Western education systems for several decades now (Kenway and Bullen, 2001; MacClure, 1989; Simon, 1988; Smyth and Shacklock, 1998), and is consistent with a shift from competency modes of pedagogic transmission to performance modes (Bonal and Rambla, 2003). Market-led reforms are based on the assumption that market forces will place pressure on schools to raise standards of performance through operational reforms as they compete for student enrolments to maintain their viability as schools. In such an educational market climate 'Competitive achievement is recognised as the core business of schools' (Teese, 1998, p. 402). Teese qualifies his statement by explaining that scholastic achievement is paramount as currency in the education market and thus can become a central focal point of school investment at the expense of a core focus on student learning and its promotion. Of course champions of neoliberal approaches to schooling contend that the performance scores are reflective of the quality of learning occurring in the schools. Although a contestable view, this is not Teese's point. Rather, it is that schools and students are encouraged to pursue and value the indicator or currency of performance over and above the learning of each individual student. Performativity can promulgate a competitive culture within education systems where performance indicators become the basis on which a school's quality is indicated and promoted, accentuating their appeal in the competitive education market. This approach has had increasing global appeal (Levin, 1998; Rizvi and Lingard, 2010) because it relieves governments of the necessity for central educational welfare and micro-management without compromising control over the system or its intended outputs. The macro implications (such as school focus and action towards market imperatives) of this systemic management approach seem somewhat obvious. Less readily apparent is the impact of education systems built on a culture of performativity for teachers' practices and students' learning, motivations, initiatives and futures at the micro level.

Notably, Teese (2000) argued that the emergence of a competitive education environment in which assessment plays a central role in establishing the conditions of comparison has increased, if not sustained, the inequitable outcomes of education for students in lower socio-economic situations in comparison to those from more affluent contexts. Consistent with this argument, Hursh (2008) reported instances where the market-orientation of the neoliberal reform agenda in the USA had increased the achievement gap between the most and least privileged students. Moreover, research from a variety of perspectives has consistently indicated that students from low socio-economic backgrounds are less likely to achieve academic success at school compared with students from high ones (Berliner, 2006; Caldas and Bankston, 1997; Knapp and Woolverton, 2004; Teese, 2000). The centrality of assessment to accountability, and administrative approaches utilising performativity within neoliberal education systems, as well as the observations of recurring systemic inequalities in educational outcomes highlight the potential work of the assessment message system as a mechanism for power and control across education, and ultimately its contribution to cultural and social reproduction (Apple, 2004; Broadfoot, 1996; Gipps, 1999). Bourdieu (1996) described the state as the primary agent in the reproduction of social order. He proposed that, through the distribution of resources and the establishment of regulatory structures, such as syllabuses and assessment regimes, state systems were able to structure populations and minds. These structures favour particular forms of organisation or being that strengthen those who conform most readily to the structure. This is not a dissimilar proposition from the recontextualising field of Bernstein's (1990) pedagogic device. The implication of Bernstein's theory of the pedagogic device with its rules and fields (see Chapter 2) is that the recontextualised knowledges or pedagogic discourses selected by education systems and employed in schools are active in the reproduction of inequalities. Assessment is particularly important in this mechanism as it consolidates both the knowledge discourse and the values associated with the discourse and then legitimates the differentiating work of the discourses through meritocratic ideological rhetoric.

While the social class effects of assessment are recognised at a general level in education sociology research, very little research has been conducted to date comparing the engagement, assessment and achievement differences between students of demographically diverse contexts in physical education. In this regard we have little information as to whether the achievement inequities between students of low and higher social class prevail in the subject or whether different patterns of participation, engagement and achievement are evident. One might assume, for example, that the status of a subject such as physical education may affect student interest and engagement where the subject's status is influenced by the pursuit by individual and school of high grades and high-status vocational futures. In this instance there may be little difference in the achievement outcomes of students in high and low SES contexts, but notable differences in who selects the subject in the schools and the academic and vocational trajectories of those students. In other words, physical education might be well populated in low SES schools, where vocational futures are less promising in comparison to the enrolment trends in high SES schools, where physical education may be viewed as a limiting factor in the pursuit of more profitable futures.

We can observe at the macro level that assessment serves as a marker of governmental and institutional interest in and value of curriculum and policy elements in the sense that officially prescribed foci of assessment are positioned as aspects of learning and practice warranting accountability. Elements of learning and practice for which accountability is not required are consequently positioned as of comparatively less significance. In some cases this differentiation is deliberate, as in the Australian example of NAPLAN, where politicians at a state and federal level were vocal in their insistence that literacy and numeracy be given prominence in the school curriculum and their desire to increase the systems' standards on the international benchmarking measures (Lingard, 2010). However, the differentiating effects can also be inadvertent where governments make public statements regarding the significance of curriculum areas such as physical education, but the absence of accountability imperatives undermines the systemically declared value of the subject and thus school investment in it. Officially sanctioned assessment can therefore be perceived as having an important bearing on the status and content of a subject. This is particularly so for physical education. As we noted in Chapter 1, several researchers in physical education have observed that current institutional investment in an accountability culture, supported by systemic assessment processes, has meant that those subjects not included in these ventures do not appear to count in the thinking of school system administrators (Rink and Mitchell, 2002). Consistent with this notion, Hardman and Marshall (2000) declared that the lower *status* of physical education across the globe seemed to be directly connected with an absence of officially sanctioned assessment. Physical education teachers themselves have associated the status of physical education with the forms of assessment expected within the subject. In Green's (2001) study, 75 per cent of teachers responding to the question, 'Why do you do examinable PE?' 'volunteered responses that had a good deal more to do with the status of PE, both internally and externally, than with pupil choice or even abstract academic justifications' (p. 60).

There are several possible responses that can be made to the perceived relationship between the status of a subject and the assessment message system. The first is to view the relationship as tenuous. This perspective rejects the notion that what is important or educationally worthwhile about a subject can or should be assessed, or that assessment can sufficiently or entirely capture the value of a subject. Such a position focuses on the unique contribution that physical education can make to the learning and life of students. The uniqueness of physical education learning opportunities and the breadth it offers to a child's overall education are promoted rather than the alignment of the subject's content with the valued features of the broader system that can be communicated through assessment expectations. A possible outcome of this perspective is that the subject will always be viewed as separate from the core business of systematic education because there is little account required or provided for its practice. It is set as peripheral and thus vulnerable to exclusion from school and system practices (Hardman, 2008). This is particularly the case where physical education is promoted as an intervention avenue for addressing the health and social problems of young people, rather than as an educative endeavour. As Evans (2004) observed, 'PE becomes easy pickings for those charged with costing education to suggest that if it isn't "physical education" that the profession is trading in, then it has no legitimate business being in schools at all' (p. 97).

An alternative approach to negotiating the intersection between systemic assessment imperatives and subject status or value has been to reform the subject in a way that sets assessment as central to the educative intentions of the subject and brings its practice in line with the practices and imperatives of other subjects, including in relation to high-stakes assessment. Langendorfer (2001) advocated such a response under the condition that the academic rigour of a physical education curriculum warrant such assessment. Queensland Senior Physical Education (Queensland Studies Authority [QSA], 2010) provides a useful example of such a response. Senior Physical Education was first developed and implemented in Queensland following an extensive review into the viability of its precursor, Health and Physical Education (HPE). The review group raised concerns about the content balance of HPE and assessment procedures in the subject (Penney *et al.*, 1997; Macdonald and Brooker, 1997a, 1997b) and advised what was to later become the QSA to break the subject into two senior examinable subjects, Senior Physical Education and Senior Health Education, in order to strengthen the content and assessment rigour of each sub-discipline. Currently in its third edition, the Senior Physical Education syllabus (QSA, 2010) defines what is one of a suite of elective subjects offered in the Queensland senior school curriculum characterised by school-based, authentic assessment that contributes to the generation of a tertiary entrance score (QSA, 2010). Physical activity serves as the orienting element for the content focus, as well as the primary site for the integrated learning and assessment of biophysical and sociocultural concepts of human movement. Since its inception in 1998, the number of students in Queensland selecting the subject has grown to over 10,000, setting Senior Physical Education as the fourth highest enrolled elective subject. The connection between 'academicised' physical education involving high-stakes assessment and increases in student enrolment numbers has also been evident in other systems, perhaps most notably in the UK, as reported by Green (2001, p. 51):

> In this vein, a recent report from the Office for Standards in Education (OFSTED) referred to 'the rapid growth of GCSE PE', which more than doubled in the 5-year period up to 1997, as 'a strong feature of secondary PE' (OFSTED, 1998, p. 1). For its part, 'A'-level PE has experienced equally swift expansion: from 35 candidates at its inception in 1985 to over 11,000 by 1998 (MacKreth, 1998) and 13,000 a year later.

Of course, this reformation of physical education has been evident and perhaps most appropriate in the context of senior schooling. However, the intentions of a senior subject are arguably distinct from those in earlier phases of learning where there may be a more convincing case for limiting formalised and graded assessment and advocating learning and engagement that is distinct from other learning areas. This continues important discussions about the purpose and constitution of physical education in general, but also draws attention to the importance of considering the role of assessment in such discussions. A second point that is necessary to consider is whether enhanced student enrolment numbers actually equates with increased status. By this, we query whether status is reflective of numbers alone, or whether there are other factors that are significant to the status of a subject that are not captured by numbers at all. For example, some subjects, such as Physics and Chemistry, have traditionally lower enrolment numbers but are generally recognised as 'high-status' subjects. In these cases status has less to do with the number of students selecting the subject and more to do with the value of scientific knowledge and discourse within the education and broader community. What is notable is that assessment is a prominent feature and expectation of learner engagement in these subjects, highlighting that assessment is central to academic value of a subject and within a subject.

Assessment value at the micro level

In most school subjects, assessment is a normal feature of students' educational experiences. Just as assessment can operate at a macro level to define curriculum value and promote adherence to particular curricular imperatives across the system, the valuing work of assessment is similarly influential at the level of the classroom and gymnasium. Within a physical education curriculum, assessment can influence how certain learning elements of the subject are viewed and engaged in by students. The way assessment is positioned and referred to by teachers has a notable impact on the way in which students view the curriculum and the elements that are of most significance. As Annerstedt and Larsson (2010) astutely observed, 'examinations define what knowledge is worthy of acquisition and mastery and also what knowledge is outside of the discipline ... what is valid knowledge in PE, therefore, involves assessment grading as an indicator of what is valuable knowledge in the subject' (p. 98). This effect of assessment is particularly acute where assessment is used by teachers as a motivational trigger through comments such as 'take note of this point, it will be on your exam'. In this regard, students apply themselves to learn and study because of impending assessment and a belief in its significance or importance, rather than because of the value of learning itself or because of an effort on the teacher's part to inspire the students' interest in the material. This can promote a performative approach to teaching and learning in schools that may work against the stimulation of students' own investment in learning. That is, the performance outcomes of assessment are set as more important than an interest and engagement in learning. Systemic performative expectations are most often the cause of such an orientation to teaching and learning. Interestingly, while notions of life-long learning are commonly promoted in education policy paraphernalia, the performative imperatives and pressures of Western education systems work against this very aspiration. The significance of other neoliberal technologies such as the marketisation of schools can have a similar impact on the performance imperatives and investments of schools and students (Kenway and Bullen, 2001). Such an effect has reportedly been more acute in private schools, where the performance outcomes of the student body are particularly important to their market appeal and viability (Locker and Croperly, 2004; Teese and Polesel, 2003).

Performativity has an impact at the micro level on both teachers and students. The professionally debilitating impact of this technology on teachers has been reported by Ball (2003), Meadmore (2001) and Jeffrey (2002), who observed that teachers had become increasingly uncertain about their work and role, felt distanced from the students and were under pressure to ensure high standards of students' work. Although the impact on students appears to have been less comprehensively studied, it is by no means less significant. Drawing on Bernstein (2000), Evans *et al.* (2004, 2005) reported data from a small qualitative study which indicated that performative pressures and what they describe as performance codes (exemplified through schools' emphases on examinations, assessment and expectations of excellence) and perfection codes (represented through specific pedagogical actions to protect unfinished bodies through intervention and prevention) contributed to the eating disorders of middle-class young women. Links between school examinations and high levels of student anxiety and depression have been commonly reported (Cole *et al.*, 1999; Hodge *et al.*, 1997), which tended to be accentuated for female students and in fee-paying comprehensive schools (Locker and Croperly, 2004). Given the potential problems of performativity for teachers and students, there is a case for resisting these pressures and associated reform practices. However, in these instances, while students may avoid the pressure for high standards and some of the consequences identified by Evans *et al.* (2004), the lack of expectation placed on students for perfection and high performances at these schools may be more detrimental to the value of the educational qualifications and educational and vocational pathways that they offer the students.

Teachers and students of physical education are generally less susceptible to the performative pressures of assessment because the accountability demands associated with the subject are considerably less than those in higher-status subjects such as Mathematics and Science. Nevertheless, assessment can be used by physical education teachers to motivate student engagement in particular facets of the subject and so perpetuate the belief that the most significant or valued features of the subject (thus warranting attention) are those that are assessed. We argue that this should not be the way assessment is utilised or referred to in physical education. Rather, assessment should be learning oriented, providing both teachers and students with useful information for the optimisation of learning and engagement in physical education.

Arguably the most poignant valuing work associated with assessment is the awarding of grades. As we mentioned in Chapter 1, although they are closely and practically linked in the reporting processes of schools, grading is not the same as assessment, but is rather a process that *uses* the information generated through assessment. The grades that are generated from the assessment and that are assigned to particular tasks and regularly reported as part of common school processes are inherently and differentially value laden. By this we mean that an 'A' standard, for example, irrespective of how it is generated, is more valued or esteemed than a 'C' standard, which is more valued than the failing grades of 'D' and 'E'. Moreover, these values (recognising that different symbols will be used in different systemic settings) are universally recognised beyond the school, even though the assessment task(s) and grading processes resulting in the assignment of the symbol are unlikely to be known by anyone other than the teachers and the students (and often the students themselves are not clearly aware of how the grades were generated). These symbols are read and utilised by those outside the school as if there is shared understanding of their meaning, even though the basis of the generation is likely to be obscure.

It is the impact on the student, and the way that students themselves are differentially valued (by the system, society, their peers and teachers) and, furthermore, *value themselves* that is the most significant outcome of this work. Several researchers have demonstrated the impact that assessment outcomes such as the reporting of grades and the consequential selection outcomes have on the way students view their own educational value and potential. For example, a student in Reay and Wiliam's often cited study declared that '*if it means you know I do badly then that means I'm gonna be a road sweeper*' (1999, p. 347). Hay and Macdonald (2010) demonstrated that the effect of assessment on the way abilities were perceived and valued also shaped the way students perceived each other and where each person 'fitted' within the social space of the physical education class. In the next chapter we consider in more detail this specific valuing feature of assessment and the impact that it has on what is viewed as ability in physical education and the mechanisms by which perceptions of the abilities of students may be constructed. Furthermore, in Chapter 5 we consider the role that these effects or consequences of assessment have on the validity of assessment in physical education.

Concluding comments

Considering assessment as a message system connected to curriculum and pedagogy is valuable from an analytical point of view. It provides a means of understanding who is privileged and who may be marginalised through assessment practices in education, generally, and in specific subjects such as physical education. More significantly, it draws attention to the specific mechanisms and valuing features of education fields that contribute to this process of differentiation of learning and learners. As we have endeavoured to demonstrate, assessment operates as a message system from the macro level right through to the micro level, defining and discriminating between the significant features of the curriculum, influencing the administration of systems, shaping educational practices with systems and subjects, and conferring value on those who are subjected to the practices. Clearly the assessment message system does not operate in isolation from the curriculum and pedagogy systems in the transmission of pedagogical knowledge, although it may well be the most influential of the three message systems.

That said, it is also important to recall Penney *et al.*'s (2009) observation that the realisation of effective learning outcomes in educational settings *depends* on the alignment and coherence of the three message systems. They demonstrated that, where one of the message systems was underdeveloped or misaligned in focus or intent, the content and effectiveness of the other message systems were affected. For example, pedagogical initiatives may be misdirected or inappropriate if effective and meaningful assessments of student performances are not made. Penney *et al.* (2009) argued that the message systems need to operate in a coherent and concerted manner. Developing this proposition further, Hay and Penney (2009) proposed that assessment could in fact be considered the most influential message system in achieving the positive intentions of the three systems together. In Chapters 7 and 8 we focus particular attention on the way in which assessment can be positioned in such a way. For this to be realised, the detrimental effects of assessment need to be understood and countered in policy and practice. In this regard, the next two chapters will focus on the impact of the valuing work of assessment in relation to the construction of students' abilities in physical education, followed by a sociocultural consideration of validity in physical education assessment. Together these two chapters will highlight the social nature and situation of assessment and focus on practices that can facilitate the unhelpful differentiating work of assessment and will offer alternative approaches that may counter the problematic consequences of assessment in order to strengthen its pedagogical value in physical education.

Part II

Enacting assessment in physical education

4 Defining, acquiring and transacting ability through assessment in physical education

Introduction

In preceding chapters we have outlined the basic premise that assessment can be viewed as a system or technology for defining and communicating value in educational settings, and demonstrated the way in which this valuing occurs in the development of systemic assessment practices and official curricular expectations. Our attention now turns to the enactment and outcomes of assessment in the classroom and, specifically, the practices of assessment in the physical education class. With this focus it quickly becomes apparent that the sites of teaching and learning are where the work of assessment to define and ascribe value is perhaps most acutely experienced by students and teachers alike. These are the contexts where teachers plan assessment tasks and programmes, collect information and make judgements about their students' progress and achievement, and report this information to various stakeholders. As several researchers have demonstrated, the experience of being assessed and the outcomes of that assessment are significant contributors to students' understanding of what is valued in a subject (Redelius and Hay, 2009), how the students themselves are valued and how they view their own value in and beyond the subject (Reay and Wiliam, 1999; Hay and Macdonald, 2008). Thinking about a physical education class from the perspective of students, we can recognise that, through participation in activities that are formally identified as assessment, tasks or 'events' signal very openly to students the relative value that is accorded to particular abilities and/or performances in physical education.

The influence of assessment on the definition and recognition of value in physical education thus also draws attention to the concept of ability. Ability in education is a concept that many people tend to take for granted. And while it is a term that is commonly used in educational settings, a coherent definition and understanding of ability is more elusive than its usage would suggest. Even at a simple level there are a variety of understandings about ability. For example, as Hay and Macdonald (2010) noted, ability can be used in a general or normative sense to describe the capacity or 'competence' of an individual or individuals to perform a task within a particular context, such as the ability to walk or the ability to swim. In contrast, ability can refer to talent, beyond the norm, such as a person who displays sporting or intellectual ability that is unusual or beyond that of the general population. Much of mainstream education literature concerned with assessment and ability focuses on this latter perspective, proffering the view that ability is a largely inherited capacity of an individual, which is modifiable to some degree because of the influence of environmental factors on its expression (Sternberg, 1998).

The general leaning towards a 'nature' explanation for differentiated ability has been historically most notable in the development of psychometric measures to determine the intelligent quotient (IQ) of individuals. Intelligence tests, fundamentally based on eugenic principles, were viewed as objective and impartial, providing accurate measures of intelligence and scholastic ability (Richardson and Johanningmeier, 1997). The application of such measures gained notable traction in Western education systems during the early to mid 1900s as they were viewed as a means by which students could be justifiably streamed into relevant educational and/or vocational avenues and thus educated according to their capacities (Shepard, 2000). Although the use of intelligence testing in schools has declined (Kornhaber, 2004), the task design principles and aspirations of the psychometricians persist in the development of contemporary systemic and standardised assessment programmes (Messick, 1994; Terwilliger, 1997), marking a distinct relationship between particular understandings of ability and the practice of assessment. The ideological premise of systemic meritocracy is underpinned by the purported objectivity of these contemporary measures and is pursued by educational bureaucrats committed to the operation of education systems where the differentiated achievement outcomes of students can be attributed to variations in students' innate capacities and efforts (Benjamin, 2003; Shepard, 2000). At a more micro level, the relationship between assessment and ability is no less interdependent and interactive. While abilities are supposed to be adequately reflected in the grades students receive following assessment episodes, it could be argued that assessment within a school subject *defines* what is considered to be ability in that subject because it defines what is valued within that site. Additionally, assessment outcomes ascribe ability levels to students in the sense that those students who receive higher grades are considered to be more 'able' than those lower-ability students who received lower grades.

Irrespective of the macro or micro context of the relationship between assessment and ability, it is clear that one's perspective on ability is inextricably linked with understandings of the 'purpose of schools, the educability and achievement potential of students, the role of teachers, the curriculum that is offered and the manner in which it is offered' (Hay and Macdonald, 2010, p. 1). Beliefs about the nature of ability inform the rationales for educational achievement and attainment differences in and through schooling (Hart, 1998), justifications for schooling reform (Davies, 1995) and current processes for identifying talent in fields as diverse as education and sport, both within and beyond schools (Gagne, 1999; Gibson *et al.*, 1999). On the significance of ability, Evans and Penney (2008) noted its inextricable link with a child's willingness and opportunity to display and receive recognition for 'ability' as well as their desire to learn in a subject such as physical education. With these realities in mind, this chapter will explore the explicit and implicit contributions that assessment practices make to the definition and transaction of what Pierre Bourdieu described as 'capital' within the fields of physical education classes, and will discuss the implications of these field dynamics for the way in which students and particular 'abilities' are variously privileged or marginalised through assessment practices in physical education.

Assessment and ability in the 'secondary field'

Bernstein identified the teaching and learning context of the education system as the 'secondary field' of the pedagogic device (1990). In relation to the secondary field, Bernstein proposed that 'This context, with its various levels, agencies, positions and practices, refers to the *selective* reproduction of educational discourse' (1990, p. 191, emphasis added). Moreover, he claimed that the secondary context of the pedagogic device 'structures the field of reproduction' (Bernstein, 1990, p. 191) and that the messages of the three systems of pedagogic transmission were *selectively* reproduced in and through the pedagogic *relationships* between teachers and learners in this field. Bernstein was asserting that, for one reason or another, official educational discourses, including those communicated through assessment expectations, are not necessarily taken up or operationalised in the classroom as may have been officially intended. Similarly, their impact upon the students within the field will not be the same or necessarily as was intended. In relation to assessment, this somewhat cursory reference to Bernstein's description of the secondary field highlights that the values operating within a physical education class as a consequence of assessment will be attributable, *in part*, to official practice expectations and discourses because they are mediated by those with power at the sites of intended implementation, whose own values, beliefs and expectations not only influence their interpretations, selections and implementations of expected assessment, but also may provide additional or alternative contributions to the dynamics and consequences of the field.

Another theorist whose academic project was not dissimilar to that of Bernstein was the French sociologist, Pierre Bourdieu, who is perhaps best recognised for his appropriation and development of the concepts of field, habitus and capital. Jenkins (2002) nicely summarised the appeal of Pierre Bourdieu's sociological concepts when he noted that Bourdieu 'is enormously good to think with' (p. 11). And, although having been critiqued for their fuzziness (or lack of empirical specificity) (e.g. Bernstein, 1996), his ideas and concepts have continued to have a marked impact on educational research, discussion and debate. We, similarly, have found the concepts of field, habitus and capital to be particularly useful in understanding and articulating the social practice and consequences of assessment. This is because of their focus on the definition and consequences of value and its obvious resonance with the valuing work and function of the assessment message system. In order to draw attention to this work we provide a brief summary of Bourdieu's most notable concepts. This is by no means a definitive commentary on his work, but rather provides a platform from which to appropriate these concepts for the purpose of describing the valuing work and consequences of assessment at the level of the secondary field.

Field is the central organising concept of Bourdieu's work. At its most basic level, a field is a site of social interaction. More specifically, it is a social arena of *relationships* and *practices* through which certain values and beliefs are situated, active and imposed on people (Wacquant, 1989). Some of the defining characteristics of educational fields are often quite obvious. These may include the syllabus requirements for learning experiences, a school's work programme, school and classroom rules, uniform requirements, etc. Other defining features such as a teacher's expectations and beliefs about physical education and physical education students can be more tacit, but no less powerful influences on the constitution of a field. A physical class could be considered a field because of the specific practices that occur in the field (teaching, learning activities) and the social interactions between all the *players* in the field (the teacher and the students). Social divisions that reflect the structured values and beliefs of the field operate so that there is an unequal distribution of power within fields. This is most clearly evident in relation to the power differential between teachers and students which can be substantiated by particular field practices such as assessment. In response to criticism of the perceived definitional ambiguity of field, Bourdieu explained that the *boundaries* of a field are situated at the point where the effects of the field on a person cease. For example, the requirements on a student in a physical education class can be seen as relatively context-specific in their influence, in the sense that the requirements do not have (and nor are they designed to have) a direct influence on the student's conduct in their Mathematics class and, because of their specificity, may in fact make no sense in a Mathematics classroom.

Bourdieu championed the term 'habitus' in reference to the lasting dispositions of a person that are evident as perceptions, appreciations, behaviours, competencies, etc. Habitus characterises the beliefs, ideals, speech, action and appearance of individuals that have been inculcated through their interactions with social agents and institutions such as schools, peers and the family (Webb *et al.*, 2002). The dispositions that make up a person's habitus are socially constructed, being acquired through historical interactions and experiences in different social contexts. These dispositions are thus reflective of the social histories and conditions in which they were acquired and largely operate below the level of consciousness. A key feature of Bourdieu's notion of habitus is its embodiment. That is, habitus is expressed or evident in the way a person appears and acts. In terms of embodiment, Shilling (1993, 2004) further explains that it 'is the experiences and appearances of the body that reveal the deepest dispositions of the habitus' (Shilling 2004, p. 475). Hunter (2004) expands this understanding of the embodiment of habitus by suggesting that the body is 'paramount in reading an individual, categorizing and positioning them within a field' (p. 176).

'Capital' offers a perspective on the ways in which a person's resources are privileged, marginalised, traded and acquired in a field (Bourdieu, 1986). The structure of the field legitimates and reproduces what personal resources (be they economic, cultural or social) may be *recognised* as capital in the field, and how it might be *transacted* for other capitals. Bourdieu identified three principal forms of capital – economic, social and cultural capital. The latter two forms of capital are perhaps less tangible than economic capital (one's financial state), but are no less significant in the impact that their possession has on the possibilities for people in social fields. Social capital can be understood as one's possession of relational networks that allow the individual to maximise their opportunities to acquire and trade other capitals (Bourdieu, 1986). For example, in a physical education setting, a student who has a strong and positive relationship with their teacher could be considered to possess more social capital than a student who is new to the class or is considered 'recalcitrant' by those with power in the field to configure or influence what is valued and sanctioned as legitimate behaviour. Bourdieu (1986) explained that cultural capital could be realised in three forms: in the *embodied* state (dispositions of the mind and body, including how one acts and looks); the *objectified* state (in the form of the possession of culturally valued goods); and in the *institutionalised* state (largely in the form of educational qualifications).

Socially constructing abilities

Several observers and researchers in physical education have applied Bourdieu's theoretical concepts of field, habitus and capital to draw attention to the way a student's ability, and indeed the notion of ability itself, is socially constructed (e.g. Evans, 2004; Hay and Macdonald, 2010; Wright and Burrows, 2006). These theoretical and empirical contributions have stood in contrast to traditional assumptions about the inherent and biological nature of ability. Evans (2004), for example, noted that physical education had become 'disembodied', reducing discussions about the nature of physical education 'to a dribble of *unproblematic assumptions* either about motivation and health-related behaviour, or "fitness", or *"talent" for "performance"* in the interest of health and/or participation in *organized sport*' (p. 96, emphasis added). He recognised that very little critical attention had been given to the concept of ability that underpinned these assumptions, or to understanding the way in which the notion of ability has been complicit in the perpetuation of inequities in physical education. In response, Evans argued that the embodied dispositions of a person's habitus could be perceived as abilities when 'defined relationally with reference to values, attitudes and mores prevailing within a discursive field' (Evans, 2004, p. 100). Further to this, Evans observed that one's identification as 'able', or 'talented', served as a form of cultural capital that could be traded for other forms of capital such as high achievement grades in a school subject.

By way of illustration (and at risk of oversimplifying what is in reality a complex and messy process), consider a physical education class as a field. In the first instance, and most obviously, the field is marked by the relationships of a teacher with students and the students with each other. Second, there are certain practices within that field that also serve as structuring features of the field. These might include, for example, dress expectations, protocols to distribute and collect equipment, typical processes for placing students into groups for practical activities, regular lesson elements such as warm ups, drills, game play and instructional practices employed by the teacher to review student performances, provide feedback and manage student behaviours. Significantly, the practices and relationships within this field establish and communicate in both tacit and overt ways certain values, beliefs and expectations that may also be considered structuring features of the field. In our example of a physical education class, values such as optimising performance outcomes, competition and aggression may be promoted through the content and modes of communication between the teacher and the students in the class. These might include certain learning activities that promote competitive engagement, feedback comments focused on performance optimisation and competition, and preferential engagement with those students who demonstrate and promote these values, beliefs and expectations in the class.

Following Evans's proposition, what constitutes or is valued as ability in the physical education class is defined by relevant structuring and value-based features of the field. Moreover, the field defines the space and context in which abilities can be legitimately displayed and recognised. That is, the dispositions, attitudes, perceptions, appearances and actions of a student's habitus are read and valued in particular ways within fields, and shape the nature of one's engagement and place in the field. For example, a muscular and keen Caucasian boy who engages in the field described above in a competitive and aggressive manner, and has an athletic appearance supplemented by the latest equipment and clothing, may be viewed as more able than either boys or girls of very different stature, or others who may have similar skills but are less assertive in the game and the field more generally. In these instances, judgements are made by the teacher, and other students, about particular students' abilities, as if they were 'natural'. In some respects this may seem an overly simplistic description of developing perceptions. Yet, considering fields as contexts in which certain transactions occur draws our attention to the operation of capital in the fields and prompts consideration of the bases and consequences of such transactions.

The structures of the fields determine the currencies and currency values for the transactions. In this regard, the elements of an individual's habitus are personal resources that operate as capital, where they are so valued. Capital can be transacted for other capital(s), used to access sites in which transactions may occur or further capital may be acquired. In the physical education class example, the muscular boy's competitive disposition and performance-oriented engagement, his athletic appearance and possession of athletic wares are embodied and objectified cultural capital, and may variously be transacted for the capital of high-ability recognition. In the first instance, however, these observations are more likely to grant him *privileged access* to the teaching and learning spaces in which ability transactions can be made and where his skills can be recognised by those positioned in the field to confer ability identification (that is, in this case, the teacher). The other students we have described have personal resources that are less likely to be recognised or transacted as ability because their appearances and/or engagement characteristics are less valued and recognised in the field. Their comparatively limited capital means that they are likely to experience greater difficulty in accessing spaces in the field where their skills can be observed, let alone be recognised as markers of their abilities in physical education. By virtue of the differential valuing of particular bodies, skills and behaviours in physical education, these students are less likely to be noticed by those who have influence in the field.

The body, Penney and Evans (2004) suggest, is of considerable significance in relation to the definition of ability in physical education. They suggest that 'particular predispositions, body shapes or "looks" clearly carry with them and are inscribed with status and meaning as valuable "physical capital", benefiting some students while alienating others' (p. 3). Furthermore, they suggest that students are 'constantly required to fabricate their "ability" in terms defined less with reference to any "real" potential, health or physical capacity than their corporeal surface features, crude indices by which "ability" is apparently displayed' (p. 4). Ability in physical education, therefore, involves the inculcation of the 'right' or legitimated physical capital (Shilling, 1993) in relation to skills, techniques and understandings (Evans, 2004), and body conscious attitudes and behaviour. It is important to acknowledge that students are themselves active and influential in shaping understandings of and experiences in physical education. In this regard, Hay and lisahunter (2006) drew attention to the contribution of students' habituses to the structuring features of fields. They observed that the behaviours and orientations of high-ability students in physical education promoted the values and structuring activities of fields that maintained their personal resources as capital, and thus their power and place as high-ability participants.

Empirical evidence for Evans's proposition of the social construction of ability was provided by Hay and Macdonald (2010), who investigated the process of ability construction by interviewing and observing one teacher and six Year-11 students (in their penultimate year of schooling) at two demographically distinct schools across 20 weeks of a school year. Over this period they collected information about the influence of teachers and students on the nature of the field, the contributing factors to ability recognition and differentiation, and the consequences of ability construction for the students in the two classes. Specifically they noted that, while the official curriculum provided an important reference point for the definition of differing levels of ability in the subject, this did not appear to be as influential as the appropriation of the official ability discourses by the teachers. It was evident that the two teachers' alignment with official discourses was individually variable depending on their own values, beliefs, expectations and histories in physical education and sport. In terms of ability recognition, physical capital was pre-eminent in both contexts, and yet it was not in itself sufficient to warrant 'high ability' identification. Recognition of a student as 'able' depended on the nature and amount of the physical capital (appearance, actual physical displays) and the affective manner of its display (such as aggression, competitiveness, hard work).

The process of ability construction had quite notable implications for the students in these physical education classes. Each student had developed a strong sense of their abilities in relation to others (where they fitted in relation to the most able, through to the least able). Bourdieu explained that habitus 'implies "a sense of one's place" but also a "sense of the place of others"' (1989, p. 19). The ease with which all the students articulated their place in the fields was testament to the significance of habitus to the nature of the field (and its divisions), but also the way the field and its practices had shaped the students' perceptions of themselves and the nature of their engagement in the classes. Moreover, as Hay and lisahunter (2006) had proposed, the habituses of individual students were contributing factors to the nature and work of the fields. In this regard, the values of the field were embodied and communicated through bodies by those who were most powerful within the field, such that they became *living criteria* against which the abilities of other students were referenced. The process of ability construction had tangible consequences for students, privileging some students and marginalising others. The high-ability students in both contexts benefited not only in the accumulation of further capital (in the form of grades), but also in the pedagogical and assessment latitude they were afforded in the fields of the physical education classes. For example, in a couple of instances the nominated 'high-ability' students were not required to demonstrate their movement capacities for assessment purposes as the teachers already presumed their high standards on the basis of previous performances and current cultural capital. For low-ability students, the process of ability construction marginalised them in the physical education fields and constrained their potential achievement such that their efforts and capacities went unnoticed or were presumed by the teacher to be of a lower standard.

Within the context of schools and schooling, Evans's notion of ability is intimately linked with the broader question of how particular conceptions of childhood development and educability, encoded within the curriculum, impact upon a child's willingness and opportunity to 'display, perform and receive recognition for "ability" in PHE classrooms, their "desire" to learn and their positioning as learners in PHE' (Penney and Evans, 2004, p. 2). Assessment is an important site of 'encoding' for and articulating competence in physical education, or for that matter any subject, and selecting for and differentiating between students who possess the codes or dispositions employed or valued within the curriculum. Where assessment is intended to capture differentiated quality, it becomes the means of defining 'degrees of ability' which may have implications for the way students understand their abilities and their future life opportunities (Lubienski, 2003). In the first instance, this points to the role of both official as well as enacted assessment practices on the nature of the field in which abilities are recognised.

The contribution of assessment to the dynamics of the field

Assessment defines the valued elements of a subject. Where official assessment expectations are set and operational in education systems (acknowledging that, in a number of systems around the world, official physical education assessment may not be well defined or even required), they draw attention to the expected knowledges and processes that students are to have acquired at a particular point in time as well as the quality of their display. These expectations are often quite succinct descriptions of the expected performance attributes of students. In Sweden, for example, these performance attributes are presented as 'Goals to Attain' by the end of a particular year of schooling (Redelius and Hay, 2009). To receive a passing grade by the end of Year 9, the Goals to Attain are (Skolverket, 2002):

- understand the relationship between food, exercise and health, and be able to apply a knowledge of ergonomics in everyday situations;
- be able to participate in games, dance, sports and other activities, and be able to perform movements appropriate to a task;
- be able to design and carry out activities for their own exercise;
- be able to orient themselves in unknown areas by using different aids, as well as be able to plan and carry out a field trip in nature during different seasons of the year;
- have a knowledge of emergency first aid;
- have a knowledge of common physical activities and how these can be performed safely.

In the National Curriculum for Physical Education in England, attainment target level descriptions provide the reference point for teachers making assessment judgements at the end of key stages. This example description for level 5 illustrates the way in which expectations are articulated in a broad manner, requiring teachers to recontextualise these valuing statements in their classroom practices:

Level 5

Pupils select and combine skills, techniques and ideas and apply them accurately and appropriately in different physical activities. When performing in different physical activities, they consistently show precision, control and fluency. They show that they can draw on what they know about strategy, tactics and composition to produce effective outcomes. They modify and refine skills and techniques to improve their performance and adapt their actions in response to changing circumstances. They analyse and comment on skills, techniques and ideas and how these are applied in their own and others' work. They explain how the body reacts during different types of activity, and why physical activity is an essential component of a healthy lifestyle. They plan, organise and lead practices and activities safely, helping others' [sic] to improve their performance.

(Department for Education, 2011)

Similarly, exit criteria and standards such as those used for Senior Physical Education in Queensland provide a notable description of the valued performance attributes of students in the subject (Hay and Macdonald, 2008). Consider, for example, the following 'Very High Achievement' statements for physical activity performance from the Senior Physical Education criteria and standards matrix.

Acquiring:
The student work has the following characteristics:

- consistent and successful reproduction of a wide range of physical responses performed fluently, accurately, and where applicable with speed
- comprehensive and accurate demonstration and understanding of rules, safety and sophisticated performance strategies through physical responses

(QSA, 2010, p. 29)

Applying:
The student work has the following characteristics:

- consistent and successful application and combination of a wide range of physical responses in authentic performance environments
- consistent and successful application and combination of a wide range of team and individual strategies that enhance the physical performances of self and others

(QSA, 2010, p. 30)

Evaluating:
The student work has the following characteristics:

- consistent and discerning reflection and decision making that enhances physical responses and outcomes in or about authentic performance contexts

- consistent and effective initiation of change or modification of personal and/or team strategies to solve problems in or about authentic performance contexts

(QSA, 2010, p. 31)

The criteria (Acquiring, Applying and Evaluating) define the properties of performance that are to be judged. The bullet point descriptors indicate the qualifying features of each property (or criterion) across five standards (Very High Achievement, High Achievement, Satisfactory Achievement, Low Achievement, Very Low Achievement). In order that the assessment judgements are 'officially' valid, physical education teachers would be required to make judgements on the learning and performances of students in the subject on the basis of these statements.

In referring to these official bases for determining levels of achievement in physical education, it is not our purpose to comment on what might be acceptable or unacceptable approaches to determining levels of achievement in physical education, but rather to highlight the way in which elements of assessment practice work to define what is valued within a particular field of judgement. This definition works to establish not only the attributes of valued performances but confers value (in the form of grades) to those who are deemed to possess the valued elements of performance. The prominence of value and the transaction that occurs on the basis of these values again renders Pierre Bourdieu's theoretical concepts of field, habitus and capital particularly useful and descriptive.

In the first instance, these statements, developed within the official recontextualising field of the pedagogic device (Bernstein, 1996), establish what could be considered the official cultural capital of the relevant physical education class. In this regard we could say that students who *possess* and *demonstrate* the valued knowledges, skills and processes represented by the official descriptions (as exemplified above) possess the official capital of the field. However, the conduct of assessment not only defines what is recognised as capital, it also serves as the process or technology through which these embodied cultural capitals may be transacted for the institutional cultural capital of a grade. More significantly, perhaps, the provision of official assessment expectations and the requirement of judgements to be made, galvanise the power and influence of the teacher over the constitution of the field so that they, in effect, become the most significant influence on what is operational as capital in the field. This provokes such questions as: What latitude for selectivity do teachers have in the assessment of their students? What official conditions of physical education practice promote the potential for selectivity? What might the implications be for the students in the field?

The extent to which official assessment expectations contribute to the construction of ability and *vice versa* depends on the extent to which the judgements made concerning the achievement levels of students are reflective of the official criteria and standards expected to be used within the physical education field. Clearly the nature of the capital that is operative within a field indicates the extent of relative contributions of official expectations and teachers' own habitus-based expectations. As was the case for ability construction, this capital will be most acutely revealed in the teachers' justification for awarding levels of achievement and, more specifically, *the evidence upon which these judgements are made*. As we will discuss in the next chapter, this is ultimately a matter of validity. The validity of all assessment relies on the quality of the evidence it generates and the interpretations that are made about that evidence (Messick, 1989). In this regard Hay and Macdonald (2008) demonstrated that the more intangible the evidence a teacher collected on student achievement (such as teachers' memories of students formed over time), the more the achievement justifications were based on value-laden affective factors (such as effort, aggression, competitiveness, etc.) rather than the content of the official criteria and standards. Similarly, in these situations, the *social capital* of the students, in terms of their connection with the teacher and connection with other students possessing embodied cultural capital, became more influential in the opportunities a student had to transact their personal resources for the institutional capital of grades. This social capital was particularly important because it granted 'wealthy' students privileged access to contexts in which their engagement and performance could be *viewed* and better *remembered* by the teachers.

Redelius and Hay (2009) demonstrated that the effects of the assessment in the field on the students in physical education classes are not benign. That is, assessment operated as a message system in quite tangible ways to communicate both what was valued in the field (irrespective of the official syllabus guidelines) and the students' own value and future within the field of physical education and movement culture more generally. Interestingly, the information generated through assessment (in particular, the grades the students received) did not appear to primarily inform students of where and in what ways they could improve 'as much as encourage them to pursue fields in which promise had already been demonstrated' (Redelius and Hay, 2009, p. 283). This implied a belief both in the naturalness of one's capacity or ability (Wright and Burrows, 2006) and the value of assessment for capturing and communicating these abilities and the appropriate futures of the students. The students in the context of this Swedish physical education study also recognised the significance of physical capital and other forms of embodied capital to high achievement in the subject. This was referred to by the students in the absence of any disgruntlement or sense of concern that such conditions might not be represented in the Goals to Attain for physical education. The physical capital was evident in relation to demonstrable performances and student appearances (the body shape and its health and fitness symbolism). Notably, however, this capital was positioned by the students as less important than displays of leadership in the class.

Concluding comments

Understanding ability and assessment through the lens that Bourdieu's concepts offer is undoubtedly helpful from an analytical point of view. It provides some reference points for the institutionalisation of values, beliefs and expectations that orient what is viewed as ability, and prompts consideration of the contribution of assessment to this process as well as the impact of existing structures on the conduct of assessment. Similarly, the concepts we have discussed in this chapter help to identify potential 'field-defining practices' that impact on the opportunities that students have to engage in meaningful, legitimate and valued ways in physical education and on the recognition of abilities and of students in physical education. Looking beyond the critical perspective that Bourdieu's concepts inevitably promote, we contend that they also provide valuable points of reference for *optimising the quality of assessment*, including limiting its unintended and negative consequences for students and the subject. For example, in recognising the impact of field, physical education teachers and those committed to optimising curriculum and assessment practices can give attention to the official and personal factors that shape what is valued in the field and how these values are instantiated in ability recognition and grading practices. From the perspective of curriculum or examination authorities, and for department or curriculum leaders in schools, it provokes consideration of official assessment guidelines and the basis for judgements, as well as articulation of necessary evidence on which to base judgements. From any individual teacher's perspective, it highlights the need for more reflexive and reflective practices where teachers are considerate of their own values, beliefs and expectations about physical education and physical education students and the ways in which these may well be expressed in and through assessment processes and practices. Our discussion points to the need for teachers to be more deliberate in the collection of relevant and reproducible evidence of 'performance quality' and the accompanying value, and indeed the necessity for assessment processes to be made clear to students such that they will have a shared understanding of the valued learnings of the field as well as equal opportunities to both acquire and apply the requisite knowledge and general capacities, and receive due and unmitigated recognition for them.

In the next chapter we draw on the concepts elucidated in this chapter on the dynamics of field, habitus and capital in the interplay between ability and assessment to offer a sociocultural perspective on validity in physical education assessment. While validity has traditionally been viewed as a psychometric principle of assessment practice, validity can be viewed from a sociocultural perspective as a necessary condition for socially just and efficacious assessment practices. In particular, a sociocultural perspective on validity directs our attention to the consequences of assessment, including those effects that have been described in this chapter. So, while it is important to consider the technical features of validity and to take the time to validate assessment techniques, we argue that this has little meaning outside a theory of validity in physical education that recognises the unique social and practical complexities of the assessment contexts, the broad intentions of the subject and the potential outcomes of practice situated within the nexus of curriculum, pedagogy and assessment.

5 A sociocultural view of assessment validity in physical education

Introduction

Any serious and considered discussion about assessment will necessarily broach the concept of validity. This is because validity is a foundational principle of all assessment practices. It is necessary for the realisation of valued assessment outcomes and the minimisation of unintended and unwanted assessment outcomes. In light of its recognised significance in general education, the absence of discussion or consideration of validity in physical education assessment is notable. Acknowledging its significance, and in response to the sparse literature currently available concerning assessment validity in physical education, the purpose of this chapter is to explain the concept of validity and its importance to practices in physical education and to draw attention to facets of practice within the field that undermine the realisation of valid assessment. Reflecting the sociocultural perspective that informs this book, the chapter directs attention specifically to the social implications and consequences of validity for physical education teachers and students and, furthermore, demonstrates the relationship between the pursuit of a socially just physical education and the optimisation of assessment validity.

At this point, it is worth reflecting on why there has been such little discussion to date about validity as it relates to assessment in the field of physical education. The most obvious reason is that physical education assessment itself has generally received less research and conceptual attention than other facets of the subject, such as pedagogy and curriculum (Hay, 2006). Similarly, as Siedentop *et al.* (2004) argued, validity has been underdeveloped in physical education as a consequence of historically shallow or menial assessment and reporting practices in the subject. These have included grading decisions made on the basis of factors such as attitudes, attendance and participation (Hensley *et al.*, 1987; Veal, 1988), as well as questionable methods for collecting evidence upon which to make meaningful interpretations of learning attainment or quality. Matanin and Tannehill (1994), for example, found that student effort was highly valued by teachers in relation to the determination of student grades. McCuaig and Hay (in press) also noted that *principled conflicts* over the purpose and constitution of the subject itself have led to inevitable difficulties in determining assessment foci and conditions of validity. To this end they argued that the impact of assessment on the potential breadth of a curriculum has run contrary to the tendency of health and physical education curriculum reformers to encompass multiple principled positions (Tinning, 2000). Thus, assessment has appeared to be a somewhat troublesome facet of practice in physical education, as committing to assessment would necessarily mean a rationalising of focus to specific principled content at the expense of others. While diverse representation is possible in curriculum documents, this is pragmatically difficult in assessment practices because of the message system's valuing and defining work.

Although some research on validity in physical education assessment has been conducted (e.g. Nadeau *et al.*, 2008; Oslin *et al.*, 1998), the focus has generally been on validating assessment tools rather than considerations of more broad and substantial notions of validity theory such as scientific inquiry (Messick, 1989) or practical argument (Kane, 2006), or the various and potentially *integrated* sources of evidence upon which field-relevant interpretations can be made. In relation to this latter point, it is arguable that such validations have been made on the basis of what some might consider to be a narrow content domain (i.e. skills and strategies in games), constraining the potential breadth and sophistication of curriculum possibilities in physical education (Penney *et al.*, 2009). Certainly, a *critical* engagement with the constitution of validity in physical education assessment has been broached in very few substantial research pieces (see, for example, Hay and Macdonald, 2008). Adding to the argument we have made throughout this book that a critical engagement with assessment is important for furthering physical education practices, we propose that understanding and considering the validity of assessment should be a central feature of this endeavour.

Understanding validity

Much of the discussion and research concerning validity in the general education literature has been situated within a positivist epistemology in the pursuit of enhanced certainty regarding the possible interpretations that can be made about the information collected through assessment. Psychometrics, the science of measurement and evaluation, exemplifies this positivist mindset towards assessment and has focused particular pragmatic attention to technical aspects of test construction. The technical qualifications of valid assessment in education literature appear overstated in comparison to the sociocultural contributions and consequences. This is, in part, a consequence of the dominating references to validity from those committed to measurement, and also of the absence of reference to validity in education research that is informed by sociocultural and critical perspectives.

This imbalance has obscured the fact that validity is much more than simply a condition for objective measures of scholarly competence. In reality, validity is relevant to *any* process involving the interpretation of observed or documented behaviours and attributes (Kane, 2001; Messick, 1998). Further-more, it is not restricted to the interpretations of task evidences, but includes the *social consequences* of the interpretations and uses of the measure (Kane, 2001; Messick, 1989, 1994, 1995). This is a key point. Validity and other subordinate but necessary conditions of assessment practice such as reliability, comparability and fairness are important to consider in relation to the employment of any educational measure as they are 'social values that have meaning and force outside of measurement wherever evaluative judgements and decisions are made' (Messick, 1994, p. 13). Informed by Messick's description of validity as a social value, a key assertion of this chapter is that validity is not merely a technical feature of assessment practice; it is a neces-sary condition for the promotion of socially just physical education, and an important consideration for anyone concerned with optimising the personal and social outcomes of a physical education.

So what is validity? Validity could well serve as an overarching condition of assessment efficacy in physical education. That is, unless the proposed assess-ment is valid (and, by implication, reliable) its use for informing decisions about future learning or learning pathways is questionable and may even be detrimental. Samuel Messick, perhaps the most influential figure in education validity theory, explained that validity is an 'integrated evaluative judgement of the degree to which empirical evidence and theoretical rationales support the adequacy and appropriateness of *inferences* and *actions* based on test scores or other modes of assessment' (1989, p.13, our emphasis). In other words, it is an evaluative summary of the evidence for and consequences of assessment practice, interpretation and use (Messick, 1995). The primary focus of validity is the interpretations that educational professionals make about the information collected through assessment. As Moss *et al.* (2006) noted, 'Educational assessment should be able to support these professionals in developing interpretations, decisions and actions that enhance student learning' (p. 109). Validity is concerned with the soundness of these inter-pretations, decisions and actions and is thus also concerned with the quality and source of the evidence that is collected.

It is important that attention is given to validity theory in physical educa-tion as validity theory 'provides guidance about what it means to say that an interpretation, decision or action is more or less sound' (Moss *et al.*, 2006, p. 109). In general, validity theories are situated within two identifiable but arguably connected churches – validity theory as scientific inquiry (e.g. Messick, 1989) and validity theory as practical argument (e.g. Kane, 2006). Generally speaking, validity as scientific inquiry involves ascertaining the extent to which defined categories of validity evidence are consistent with the inferences and actions that are made and establishing that alternative inferences are less likely. This latter element involves the testing of plausible rival hypotheses relating to particular categories of validity evidence that is collected (Messick, 1989; Moss *et al.*, 2006). In seeking what he argued was a more pragmatic approach to validity, Kane (2006) proposed that validation involved two kinds of argument: an *interpretive argument* and a *validity argument*. The interpretive argument sets out 'the network of inferences and assumptions leading from the observed performances to the conclusions and decisions based on the performances' (p. 23). Following this process, the validity argument provides an overall judgement on the coherence of the interpretative arguments based on the logical and empirical evidence that has been collected.

Although variations of validity theory such as Kane's theory as practical argument have been proposed in educational discourse, Messick's notion of construct validity is generally viewed as the most comprehensive and generative conceptualisation. Indeed the variations of validity theory more often than not are referenced from or build upon Messick's proposal. Messick argued that the content, criteria and consequences of assessment could be integrated into a *construct* framework against which the validity of any educational measure or judgement could be referenced. Messick specified construct validity in relation to six elements which all need to be met to satisfy the conditions of validity. These were: content, substantive, structural, generalisability, external and consequential. Each element provides a complementary form of evidence that, when integrated, may produce an overall judgement of construct validity. In this regard, validity is a matter of degree, not an all-or-nothing property of an educational measure (Kane, 2001; Messick, 1989). For construct validity to be assured in physical education, attention needs to be given to the content relevance and representativeness of the planned tasks to the physical education domain content (content); a clear alignment of task processes and the characteristic processes of the subject domain (substantive); the development of scoring or grading approaches (e.g. criteria and standards) that are reflective of task and domain structure (structural); a balance between task depth and construct coverage, and an assurance of inter- and intra-rater reliability (generalisability); convergent and discriminate correlations of the assessment scores with external variables such as the accountability interests of education systems (external); and an investigation of the positive and negative, intended and unintended, consequences of the task and its outcomes for physical education students (consequential).

Focusing on the consequences

Without a doubt, Messick's final condition of construct validity, consequences, has been his most debated (Kane, 2001; Markus, 1998; Moss, 1998). The notion of consequences as validity evidence refers to the importance of taking into account the *effect* of assessment and its outcomes on students. Messick (1989) claimed that the validity of an assessment task and its interpretations were compromised *either* by the failure to realise the intended outcomes (learnings or behaviours) *or* if other unintended outcomes were inordinately engendered by the assessment task or its interpretations. For example, if the intention of a task is for a particular concept to be learnt, it is necessary in the first instance to establish whether that concept has been learnt or not and whether the task sufficiently supported the realisation of that learning. More controversial has been Messick's insistence that unintended learnings that occur as a result of the assessment task or its associated outcomes (e.g. the grading of students) compromise the validity of the task. Such unintended learnings may include the development of perceptions about students' selves, their value and the value of their capacities (and perhaps, particularly in physical education, one's body, its desirability, capacities and capabilities). Problematic outcomes of assessment such as these were exemplified by research conducted by Reay and Wiliam (1999), who reported that assessment had quite influential consequences for students' perceptions of their own capacities and the capacities of others for learning, as well as their likely futures. They reported one student who stated, '*you have to get a level like a level 4 or a level 5 and if you're no good at spellings and times tables you don't get those levels and so you're a nothing*' (p. 345). In these instances assessment outcomes can perpetuate unhelpful beliefs about a person's self and make a significant contribution to the formation of their identity.

Those troubled by the notion of consequential validity query whether it is possible to determine the unintended consequences of assessment or whether teachers and tasks should be held to account for the way assessment experiences and grades are interpreted by those who participate in or receive them. Reay and Wiliam (1999) and Jones and Myhill (2004) reported that in fact teachers make very tangible contributions to students' meaning-making of assessment and its outcomes, particularly where their own professional standards are tied to the achievement outcomes of their students. Teachers can preface engagement in assessment by highlighting how important the assessment is to students' futures, the standard of the class, the school, etc. Similarly, unintended and unhelpful consequences of assessment can flourish in the absence of debriefing after the assessment has been conducted and the students have received their grades. Teachers need to help students to use the information derived from the assessment constructively so that they are less likely to define themselves and their futures by false assumptions of a symbol's significance (i.e. a grade) and more likely to positively engage with and utilise provided feedback. This is to say that the assessment work of a teacher does not end with the awarding of a grade. Teachers must teach students to make helpful, realistic and appropriate sense of the assessment and its implications for them.

Our purpose for specifically focusing on the issue of consequential validity is threefold. First, consequential validity draws attention to the potential negative consequences of assessment in physical education such as a student's diminished sense of capacity in the subject and their disconnect with physical culture beyond the classroom. If assessment in physical education contributes to negative and unintended learnings such as these, then its development and employment in the subject must be rigorously reviewed. All too often in mainstream education, differences in student achievement is attributed to the meritocratic claims of student ability and effort (Benjamin, 2003; Hart, 1998) rather than problems with the measures used to generate the achievement which feeds into students' beliefs about their 'natural' capacities and suitable futures. The physical education community has to be wary of this tendency and give due care and attention to socially just assessment practices. Second, consequential validity requires physical educators to take greater interest in and account for the outcomes of assessment in addition to those responsibilities and accountabilities related to the design and implementation of assessment. This interest and accountability has quite a practical implication for physical education teachers, including active assessment debriefing with students and the necessary development of students' *assessment literacy* (see Chapter 6). Third, consequential validity draws attention to the potential pedagogical work of assessment (Tinning, 2009). Tinning described pedagogical work as being constituted by two key characteristics. He argued that, if there was no explicit intention to pass on knowledge by someone (teacher, coach, parent, other pedagogue) by various pedagogic means (including teaching and coaching but also, for example, use of social media), then no pedagogical work has been 'done'. Pedagogical work is thus clarified as a *consequence* of pedagogical *intentions* (Tinning, 2009). We propose that the obvious link between consequential validity and pedagogical work (intention and consequence) provokes teacher consideration of the reasons for conducting assessment, effective communication of these intentions and the concerted ascertainment of the extent to which they have been realised. Again, the challenge is to determine what the effects of assessment are. This requires teachers who are both reflective and reflexive practitioners (Hay and Macdonald, 2008) and who are committed to physical education assessment that is equitable, inclusive and thus socially just.

Validity as a necessary condition of socially just physical education

Validity is primarily concerned with the interpretations that are made about the information collected through assessment. The quality and utility of these interpretations for all students depends upon the fairness and equity of the measures. In this regard, the validation of an assessment task or programme requires that all students have equal access to sites for and of assessment, the judgement of performance in the absence of construct-irrelevant factors such as a student's appearance or disposition and considerations of the consequences of assessment for students' learning, perceptions of themselves and their ongoing engagement in a movement culture. This concern for equity of opportunity and outcomes in the absence of prejudice are, likewise, fundamental to a social justice agenda in physical education.

In developing this link between validity and social justice further, it is helpful to unpack the notions of fairness and equity. Both are important facets of validity but have been somewhat sidelined in validity discussions because of a preoccupation with the technical or scientific imperatives of the process. Stobart (2005) argued that 'fairness is fundamentally a sociocultural, rather than technical, issue' (p. 275) of assessment and that 'fair assessment cannot be considered in isolation from both the curriculum and educational opportunities of the students' (p. 275). What needs to be fair in assessment is access to educational opportunities, as much as equal opportunities to be assessed under the same conditions. In this way fairness and equity can to some extent be considered to be of the same order. Yet, equity also prompts us to consider the nature of the opportunities to which access is granted. From a social justice and equity perspective, 'opportunities' are not neutral. Thus, the notion of fairness prompts recognition that discrepancies in students' access to both content and experiential opportunities leads to educational injustice where students are assessed under the assumptions that their opportunities have been the same. Such assumptions lead to the conclusion that the differences in student achievement are inherent. If the students' opportunities have not been the same, then the assessment and its assumed meritocratic outcomes are unjust. But pursuing equity requires that the opportunities themselves are problematised. By this we mean that disadvantage and privilege are inherent in the content and nature of 'educational opportunities' that curriculum, pedagogy and assessment individually and collectively provide. Thus, efforts towards the promotion of socially just physical education assessment also requires that attention be directed to the focus and nature of the content itself and the valued ways of demonstrating learning through assessment.

Social justice is a term that has been widely employed in education literature. North (2008) lamented, however, that its use has largely lacked theoretical coherence and reflected populist conceptualisations and rhetorical idealism. Wary of this criticism but convinced of its importance to physical education, we propose that the assurance of assessment validity is a necessary element of facilitating socially just education experiences in physical education. The dual dimensions of social justice proposed by Gerwitz (1998) serve as a useful point of definition and reference. Gerwitz (1998) conceptualised social justice in relation to a distribution dimension and a relational dimension. Distribution justice refers to the principles by which material and symbolic resources (such as rights, duties, and social and economic goods) are distributed in society, and is concerned with equality of opportunity and equality of outcome. Relational justice attends to issues of power and the treatment of others, and specifically refers to 'the nature and ordering of social relations, the formal and informal rules which govern how members of society treat each other both on a macro level and at a micro interpersonal level' (Gerwitz, 1998, p. 471). While perhaps analytically distinct, these two dimensions are interdependent. For example, gender equity in access to positions of authority in schools depends on the power relationships between agents in that setting and the implicit structuring of roles and identity as a consequence of those relationships.

Physical education that is socially just should reflect both the distribution and relational dimensions described by Gerwitz in relation to curriculum content (Azzarito and Solomon, 2005), pedagogical engagement (Hunter, 2004) and assessment (Hay and Macdonald, 2008). As we have emphasised, these three elements or message systems of education are interdependent, and the relationship can and should be observed in the notion of validity. In fact, it would be reasonable to propose that the pursuit of a socially just physical education assessment *requires* the assurance of validity. For example, the fair access of students to contexts within physical education that provide for the display and recognition of learning is also a necessary condition for generating quality information from which valid interpretations can be made. However, this information can be affected by students' disproportionate access to equipment, the different positions that students assume or are 'assigned' by teachers or other students in the social field of a physical education class, the power imbalances between students, the observational preferences of teachers and so on. In these instances, more information may be collected about some students and less about others. However, if the information cannot be shown to be relevant or equally representative of all students in a cohort, the interpretations that can be made at the level of the cohort are restricted. Even the meaning of the graded outcomes of assessment are rendered somewhat spurious as the differences in achievement cannot be adequately attributed to performance alone, having been inordinately affected by differences in the quality of information collected for each graded student.

Efforts to enhance the validity of assessment in physical education, then, will involve teachers giving attention to distributional and relational dimensions of classroom practice. Attention to distributional justice in assessment will particularly focus on ensuring that all students have had access to learning opportunities in physical education and that their opportunities to display this learning for assessment are equitable. As we suggested earlier, this aspect of socially just practices first requires consideration and problematisation of 'opportunity', including unpacking the disadvantages and privileges afforded by the content of the subject itself. That said, practically, we propose that a key feature of assessment that is 'distributionally just' is the generation of reproducible and accessible evidence of every student's physical education learning. We will comment further on this later in this chapter. In terms of relational justice, efforts need to be made by teachers to enhance the power of the students within the teacher–student assessment relationship. In Chapter 6 we propose that a promising approach to addressing the inherent power imbalance of assessment is to increase the *assessment literacy* of students and raise their expectations of both the teacher's practice and their experiences of assessment. This involves providing them with greater understanding of the conditions of *assessment efficacy* (Chapter 7) as well as knowledge of how to use assessment information productively for their own learning.

Perhaps as a consequence of their paradigmatic distinctions, the relationship between validity and a social justice agenda has remained either unacknowledged or unexplored in physical education and education literature. This is both a conceptual and practice oversight that needs to be better resolved to optimise the education outcomes for all students. The validity of assessment in physical education should be a key interest of those conducting assessment and those committed to a meaningful physical education for all students. Failing to make it so can allow unhelpful ideas about one's capacities and place within a broader movement culture to take root. Instead of promoting and supporting the engagement of all students in movement experiences and ongoing learning in movement contexts, assessment may serve to affirm those who are already committed to such engagement and alienate those whose grades are misinterpreted as indicating their questionable legitimacy in movement fields.

Evidence and interpretations in physical education

Having drawn attention to validity theory, and in particular to the implications of construct validity for assessment in physical education, our intention is not to affirm one theory over another for the subject, but rather to provoke consideration about the specific nature of validity in physical education assessment. This said, we do believe that assessment development and practice in physical education should meet certain conditions. In Chapter 7 we present four interdependent conditions for assessment efficacy in physical education that are situated within an expectation of aligning the planning and implementation of curriculum, pedagogy and assessment. Consistent with our sociocultural perspective on assessment, these conditions include assessment that is learning-oriented, authentic, valid and socially just. One of the practical implications of these conditions of efficacy is that we advocate assessment that is contextually relevant and that integrates elements of the psychomotor and cognitive domains of learning. Such assessment approaches have been variously viewed as performance assessments, authentic tasks, educative assessments, etc. (recognising, of course, that the content of such tasks will vary depending on one's view of curriculum content and integration in the subject). In relation to assessment that is based in more constructivist views on learning, Gipps (1994) claimed that Messick's definition of validity 'takes us firmly into a scenario in which educational and social implications of assessment are addressed' (p. 69). Indeed, international and domestic changes in assessment approaches from traditional tests to more authentic and learning-oriented assessments have maintained validity as a fundamental aspect of practice, emphasising 'the appropriateness of assessment tasks as indicators of intended learning outcomes, and … the appropriateness of the interpretation of assessment outcomes as indicators of learning' (Cumming and Maxwell, 1999, p. 177).

However, the increased contextual and practical complexities of these assessment tasks have implications for the nature and defence of their validity (Bachman, 2002; Messick, 1995). As Bachman (2002) identified in relation to language performance assessments, 'with greater opportunity for this richness of attributes to be involved, the process of demonstrating the validity of intended inferences about specific areas of language ability … becomes more difficult' (p. 5). The richness, complexity and associated difficulties for validating assessment are accentuated in physical education because of the inherent variations and fluidity of movement contexts in which authentic physical education assessment will take place. In recognition of this added complexity, Nadeau *et al.* (2008) observed that 'proper assessment of the students' progress may be very challenging for PE teachers, faced with the use of appropriate measurement techniques for areas as diverse as the cognitive domain, the psychomotor domain or the physical development domain' (p. 66). Quality (or valid) interpretations can only be made on the basis of quality information which itself is necessarily generated through quality processes. Thus, concerns for validity in physical education direct our attention to the construction and implementation of assessment, and the selection of information for interpretation (Nadeau *et al.*, 2008), as much as the outcomes and uses of the information that is generated in order to make sense of the information collected in the complex contexts described above. As we mentioned above, the contexts for meaningful and authentic assessment in physical education are more complex and thus require careful consideration as to the forms and meanings of the information they generate. With this in mind there are certain informational characteristics that are necessary to support valid interpretations.

Fundamentally, the information that is collected needs to be *reproducible* and *accessible* to both students and teachers. This is comparatively simple in pen and paper tests or written tasks where teachers and students have access to tangible texts and associated feedback comments. However, it is more difficult in psychomotor domains where the movement contexts and associated performances are fleeting and most often captured by the observations of teachers. Hay and Macdonald (2008) reported that the absence of reproducible evidence in a senior physical education subject resulted in the teachers' reliance on memory as the most common form of evidence for making grading decisions. They observed that the teachers made observations of students' physical performances across time, but most clearly remembered the performances of the students whose dispositional and physical characteristics were most like their own. Similarly, they remembered the students who were most inconsistent or contrary to their values, beliefs and expectations of physical education and physical education students. The validity of the grading interpretations that the teachers made was compromised on a number of fronts. In particular, the prominence of observation and memory facilitated the inordinate intrusion of construct-irrelevant factors such as the values, beliefs and expectations of the teachers on the evidence collected and interpreted by the teachers. Additionally, the dispositional factors such as students' enthusiasm and competiveness enhanced their access to contexts for assessment recognition at the expense of opportunities accessible to less assertive students, so that the volume of evidence that was collected (questionable as it may have been) was not equal for all students.

The validity of assessment in physical education has also been shown to be influenced significantly by a lack of clear definition of the constructs and learning domains being assessed, and in particular a lack of communication of these constructs to the students. Not only does this result in questionable interpretations that can be made by the teachers about the questionable assessment 'evidence' they have collected, but the outcomes of such interpretations can include students' misunderstandings about the values and focus of physical education itself. Redelius and Hay (2009), in demonstrating the communicative effects of the assessment message system on physical education and health students in Sweden, noted that the teachers' own absence of attention to the official bases for collecting and interpreting assessment information, while in and of itself fostering disruptions to the content and structural validity of the assessment practices, led to students' significant misunderstanding of the goals of physical education and the nature of their expected engagement in the subject. Moreover, it led to an emptying of the knowledge expectations of the subject and an increased prominence of dispositional and affective characteristics (Redelius and Hay, 2011). These findings were supported by Annerstedt and Larsson (2010, p. 111), who observed that 'teachers cannot explicitly articulate criteria for how and what they grade and there exists a large amount of variance in grading related to lack of validity and reliability in the grading situation'. Moreover, like Redelius and Hay (2009), they concluded that 'if students are not explicitly taught how to meet these informal and implicit demands with regards to grading it will create a lack of transparency, inequality, uncertainty, unfairness as well as poor comparability between schools' (Annerstedt and Larsson, 2010, p. 111). In summary, clear, consistent and demonstrable alignment between the official bases for collecting and interpreting assessment information and teacher practice is needed to limit construct-irrelevant practices and judgements and to optimise the intended learning outcomes of the students, including their understanding of the relationship between expected learning and assessment.

Optimising physical education assessment validity

In order to optimise assessment in physical education it is important that attention is given to the factors that affect the degree to which valid interpretations and actions can be made. In the first instance, as we will describe in more detail in Chapter 6, teachers need to be *assessment literate*. It is impossible to expect assessment practices to be valid if those developing, implementing and interpreting the assessments are not aware of the conditions of validity or of assessment as a central feature of physical education practices. In many cases this will require that pre-service physical education teachers and practising physical education teachers engage in specific courses or professional development opportunities that are focused on matters of validity. For both pre-service and practising teachers, these learning opportunities should involve instruction on validity theory; processes for the collection of construct- and domain-relevant evidence; the relationship between official reference points for decision making (often criteria and standards) and the evidence that has been collected; and the communication of assessment information and interpretations to students (including debriefing students in order to limit unintended learnings associated with assessment and its outcomes). We believe that the should also include the promotion of teachers' reflexivity to address the source and nature of construct-irrelevance in the collection and interpretation of assessment information. In this case we refer to the self-analysis of one's beliefs, values, history, etc. in recognition that these aspects unavoidably influence one's perceptions of others and their interactions with them. This approach may aid teachers in understanding the influence they have over student achievement and opportunity to achieve and help them develop pedagogic and assessment strategies that address the problematic consequences of such influence.

Systemically, in order to ensure the viability of alternative assessments that employ teacher judgements, attention needs to be given to the nature and clarity of the official assessment guidelines that teachers are provided with (specifically what and how progressive judgements of students' performances are to be made, stored and accounted for) and support given for teachers' interpretations of these expectations in practice. This could be through the provision of example assessment approaches, indicative standards of students (housed electronically online) and example forms of feedback and justification. Moreover, we argue that greater transparency in the decision-making processes of physical education teachers is needed to enhance both the distributional and relational justice of their practices. Specifically, this could involve the statutory requirement for teachers to give greater justification to each student for the referencing decisions they make. In this regard it would be unacceptable to simply provide students with an unexplained grade, requiring that students be made aware of both the reasons for the grade and the implications for future learning in the subject.

Of course, greater justification for assessment decisions needs to be made on the basis of defensible evidence of student learning that has been systematically collected on every student, and on the basis that this evidence is accessible to every student. We recommend that in the psychomotor domain video evidence provides the most accessible and generative feedback opportunities for teachers and students. Current advances in technology have made the collection, storage and retrieval of video evidence a much more feasible option than has been the case in the past. Many students themselves have access to videos on their mobile phones that can allow for the collection of their own performance evidences, both within and external to the classroom context (Penney and Hay, 2008). Similarly, small, hand-held, high-definition cameras with USB connectivity are available on the market at relatively low cost. School physical education departments could purchase class sets so that teachers and students could easily and regularly collect evidence of integrated performances for both formative and summative purposes. In relation to our concern for validity, this enhances the likelihood that evidence is collected on all students and that students increase their understanding of evidence and its use in the facilitation of their learning.

Concluding comments

Informed by a sociocultural perspective on assessment in physical education, in this chapter we have sought to understand validity and its impact not only on the usefulness of discrete assessment tools, but also on physical education students and the subject itself. We endeavoured to demonstrate that the establishment of valid assessment in physical education requires more than just the validation of assessment techniques (although this is important). It requires concerted attention to the intersections and integrations of curriculum, pedagogy and assessment to ensure that the values being communicated through assessment are readily accessible and consistent with the official and intended curricula in which students are engaged. The validating work that has already been conducted in physical education is important and has raised useful considerations about what should be captured in assessment and what interpretations should be made. However, there is much more to be understood regarding the theory of validity in physical education and the way in which the validity of assessment has been undermined in many contexts through ignorance, by trivial assessment practices or by the disconnection of assessment with pedagogy and curriculum, especially where assessment is planned apart from these elements of practice or merely tacked on the end of a unit of work to meet some bureaucratic reporting expectations. Returning to Messick's (1994) assertion that validity is a social value that has meaning and influence outside the task for those engaged in assessment and affected by its outcomes, we implore the physical education community to consider the consequences of assessment as part of efforts towards strengthening the validity of assessment.

In the next chapter we draw on the theoretical and conceptual material we have developed in Part I of this book to begin to consider how assessment can be positioned and promoted in physical education in such a way as to limit the problematic outcomes of assessment and to facilitate valued learning in the subject. Thus, we seek to draw instruction from the critical perspectives that have informed our sociocultural perspective on assessment, including its contribution to the work and outcomes of the pedagogic device and its operation as a message system, to propose assessment principles underpinning practices that can make a notable contribution to the educative aspirations of physical education.

6 Assessment literacy in physical education

Introduction

Continuing to utilise Bernstein's concepts as a prompt, we recall that central to the operation of the pedagogic device and the work of message systems is the transmission and receipt of educational discourses. Bernstein thus recognised that agents within the education context, including teachers and students, receive information of varying orders that has to be decoded, interpreted, recontextualised and applied in specific school, classroom and pedagogical settings. Teachers and students operating within the message systems thus receive and make sense of information that is communicated to them via various means and will then act on, apply and communicate their interpretations of that information in the contexts and conditions in which they are working. For example, physical education teachers are required to interpret the curriculum and assessment expectations of syllabus documents and in turn communicate this information to students through the implementation of unit or lesson plans and assessment programmes. Similarly, students engage in assessment tasks and programmes that require them to read, interpret and understand what is expected of them and to produce responses (movement and/or written) that accord with the assessment expectations. While in some instances the communication channels and means may be easily recognisable, Bernstein's work repeatedly drew attention to the complex and subtle ways in which discourses could be seen to 'operate' and gain legitimacy and dominance in education. In this chapter we pursue these issues as they relate to assessment in physical education and, more specifically, the notion of *assessment literacy*.

In lay terms, *literacy* refers to the ability to read and write. Marginally more generative definitions present literacy as a person's knowledge or competence in a particular field of endeavour. This latter understanding of literacy is what generally informs the notion of *assessment literacy*. In this chapter we adopt, explore and extend this term as a means of drawing attention to the machinations and potential consequences of the sorts of processes alluded to above, involving both teachers and students making sense of and endeavouring to respond to assessment requirements and tasks in physical education. Assessment literacy, as the term has been utilised in general education literature over the past 20 years (see, for example, Fullan, 2000; Popham, 2006; Stiggins, 1991, 1999), describes teachers' understanding of assessment processes as well as their capacities to design assessment tasks, develop adequate criteria for making valid judgements on the quality of students' performances, and understand and act upon the information that is collected through assessment. More specifically, the term assessment literacy has been popularly employed in the USA to refer to 'the collective capacity of teachers and the principal to examine student performance data, to make critical sense of it in the disaggregate, to develop action plans based on the data, and to take action that is monitored' (Fullan, 2002, p. 412). Popham's (2006) view similarly focuses on the capacity of teachers to interpret test data as a fundamental element of assessment literacy. He argued that the absence of such capacity within the teaching profession was 'astonishing in light of the fact that during the last 25 years, educator competence has been increasingly determined by student performance on various large-scale examinations' (2006, p. 84).

The rise of national and international standardised assessment endeavours and their potential misuse by governments and other societal agencies (such as the media) prompted Taylor (2009) to contend that assessment literacy needed to be developed across a more diverse set of test stakeholder groups. In Taylor's view these included teachers and parents as well as school administrators. Similar to Fullan and Popham, Taylor advocated the development of teachers' assessment literacy that allowed them to be productively engaged in 'selecting, administering, interpreting, and sharing results of large-scale tests produced by professional testing organizations' (2009, p. 24). Yet, Taylor's expectations of teachers' assessment literacy continued beyond the interpretation and consequential actions associated with performance scores to teachers 'developing, scoring, interpreting, and improving classroom-based assessments' (2009, p. 24). Taylor's comments pointed to the need for teachers to be able to critically engage with forms of assessment and specific instruments that in many education systems have attained seemingly unquestionable status and authority, and to be able to develop assessments that can meet specific educational needs in a particular pedagogical context.

Recognising the significance of formative assessment, Popham (2009) again offered a broader framework for describing assessment literacy that included 'classroom assessments' and 'accountability assessments'. In terms of *classroom assessments*, assessment literacy thus referred to a teacher's capacity to identify and employ appropriate measures in their classes and make appropriate interpretations of the information generated by such measures. While there may be an understandable tendency to envisage quantitative 'standardised' measures here, a key aspect of assessment literacy conceived in this way is teachers' abilities to recognise and engage with qualitative data and, in so doing, gain a measure of student learning. In relation to *accountability assessments*, Popham's notion of assessment literacy focused on a teacher's understanding of the characteristics of effective measures and the capacity to identify technical errors in task construction and to make useful meaning of the performance outcomes generated by such measures.

As indicated above, we agree that assessment literacy is important for all teachers to develop, including physical education teachers. While systemic, large-scale, standardised measures are less common in physical education across the world, we contend that, as members of the broader teaching profession, physical education teachers need to be conversant in the language of assessment, encompassing both classroom and accountability assessment. Moreover, we concur with Taylor (2009) and Popham's (2009) expectations that teachers need to be sufficiently knowledgeable in assessment practices in order to select, construct and implement meaningful assessment tasks and programmes and make coherent and productive interpretations of this information. However, we believe that, while undeniably important, this emphasis alone is inadequate to describe the necessary capacities for engagement in the assessment message system. Furthermore, assessment literacy as conceptualised and described by Taylor (2009) and Popham (2009) fails to acknowledge that developing assessment literacy *is as much a necessity for students as it is for teachers.* In part these weaknesses are attributable to a somewhat narrow appropriation of literacy. Before returning to notions of assessment literacy for teachers and students in physical education, we therefore turn our attention to what we view as a more conceptually generative understanding of literacy.

Conceptualising literacy

Although a relatively common term, literacy is a broad and contested concept in the general education literature. In contrast to the simple definitions offered at the beginning of this chapter, Freebody and Luke (2003) posited a definition of literacy that expanded its instantiation from one's capacity to read and write to 'the extent to which people and communities can take part, fluently, effectively and critically, in the various text- and discourse-based events that characterise contemporary semiotic societies and economies' (p. 53). Further, they argued that such a conception of literacy draws attention to three aspects of literate practice. First, they nominated the 'extent' of practice, describing this as the 'widely varying and varied levels of fluent, effective and critical practice that individuals and communities have access to and engage with' (p. 53). Second, they drew attention to the breadth of an individual's or community's textual repertoire. Finally, they argued that their definition of literacy emphasised that societies and communities are heterogeneous with 'diverse and hybrid identities and practices, texts and media' (p. 54). What is important to note here is that the capacity to actively participate in a social field is fundamental to what it means to be literate. Furthermore, Freebody and Luke draw our attention to the fact that the contexts of participation are complex and diversely constituted, in the sense that they are influenced by people with varied social and cultural experiences, beliefs, expectations, motivations and communicative capacities, as well as by structural conditions ranging from policy expectations through to the spaces or environments of engagement.

Reflecting these aspects of literate practice, Freebody and Luke (1990, 2003) proposed the 'four roles' model of literacy 'as a set of specifications for literacy pedagogy, curriculum and assessment' (2003, p. 56). These four roles of effective literacy included:

- *Breaking the code of texts*: Recognising and using fundamental features and architecture of written texts, including: alphabet, sounds in words, spelling, punctuation, conventions and patterns of sentence structure, page layout, directionality and text formatting.
- *Participating in the meanings of text*: understanding and composing meaningful written, visual and spoken texts in ways that connect texts' meaning systems to people's available knowledges and experiences of other cultural discourses, texts and meaning systems, and the relevant and purposeful inferences that can be drawn from these connections.
- *Using texts functionally*: traversing and negotiating the social relations around texts; knowing about and acting on the different cultural and social functions that various texts perform both inside and outside school and knowing that these functions shape the way texts are structured, their tone, their degree of formality and their sequence of components, and the courses of social action they can accomplish with particular texts.
- *Critically analysing and transforming texts*: understanding and acting on the knowledge that texts are not transparent windows on the world, that they are not ideologically natural or neutral, that they represent particular views and silence others, influence people's ideas; and that their designs and discourses can be critiqued and redesigned in novel and hybrid ways.

(Freebody and Luke, 2003, pp. 56–57)

A direct transfer of the four roles model of literacy to a notion of assessment literacy is not altogether tenable. However, Freebody and Luke's work prompts recognition that literacy is not merely a technical quality of engagement or communication, but also an inherently social and socially constituted practice. As we argue throughout this book, this is also the case for assessment. Freebody and Luke's work thus serves as a basis from which to reconceptualise the notion of assessment literacy to more accurately reflect the sociocultural contexts, practices and outcomes of assessment for all 'players' in the fields of engagement, rather than focusing merely on the knowledge and practices of teachers.

Reconceptualising assessment literacy

In the first instance, the four roles model of literacy leads us to consider assessment as a particular text, or as being characterised by certain textual features. Some of these textual features are obvious. For example, 'official' requirements for assessment in physical education and the associated process and foci expectations are most often contained in texts (such as syllabuses) and require interpretation by teachers. Similarly, assessment tasks and movement performance expectations are communicated by teachers to students either verbally or through task sheets, requiring students to comprehend these expectations and produce commensurate performances. The students' performances are themselves texts, whether in a written, oral and/or movement form and, as such, are 'read' and interpreted by the teacher and other students. In many ways these are obvious facets of the literate engagement of teachers and students with assessment tasks and outcomes, and between each in relation to the enactment of assessment. However, as noted in our opening chapter, assessment also communicates more covert messages that are recognised to varying degrees by students, and that carry and convey disproportionate consequences for those students whether the messages are recognised or not. As we demonstrated in Chapter 4, these covert or implicit features of field-situated discourses are central to the valuing process of those fields and may have significant implications for the grades that students receive and the perceptions they develop of their abilities in physical education.

Recognising the textual nature and features of assessment and the associated discourses that are both overtly and covertly communicated in and through the practice of assessment strengthens the argument for a broader notion of assessment literacy. Failing to view assessment literacy in relation to both the technical and the sociocultural aspects of practice, or from the perspective of both teachers and students, has the potential to undermine the value and significance of assessment in physical education. With this is mind we propose that assessment literacy can be viewed in relation to four interdependent elements:

- *Assessment comprehension* – focusing on knowledge and understanding of assessment expectations and conditions of efficacy.
- *Assessment application* – focusing on the conduct of assessment in terms of either teacher implementation or student engagement.
- *Assessment interpretation* – focusing on making sense of and acting on the information that is collected through assessment practices, including traversing and negotiating the social relations of assessment.
- *Critical engagement with assessment* – focusing on awareness of the impact or consequences of assessment and challenging the 'naturalness' of assessment practices, performances and outcomes.

The interdependence and joint representation of these four elements is fundamental to the realisation of assessment literacy. By this we mean that the possession or demonstration of one element or the absence of one or other elements compromises a person's level of assessment literacy. For example, technical knowledge of appropriate assessment techniques is of limited merit if one's implementation of assessment practices is questionable. Similarly, a critical perspective on assessment and its outcomes in the absence of assessment knowledge and practice does little to improve the experiences of students or counter the unhelpful discriminating consequences of assessment. As we have argued, both physical education teachers and students need to be assessment literate. In the next sections we elaborate on the specifics of these four elements of assessment literacy as they relate to physical education teachers and to students.

Assessment literacy for physical education teachers

The key focus of assessment literacy for teachers is the development of knowledge and capacities to implement assessment and interpret the outcomes of assessment in a manner that is critically aware and that optimises the value of assessment for all students (as described below). This requires that teachers possess technical capacities for conducting assessment as well as a broader understanding of the sociocultural conditions and consequences of assessment and the teacher's contribution to these processes.

Assessment comprehension

Broadly, assessment comprehension for teachers focuses on their knowledge of assessment in educational contexts. It draws attention to teachers' understanding of the conditions of assessment efficacy (see Chapter 7). As we have proposed elsewhere (Hay and Penney, 2009), these conditions focus on understanding the purposes of assessment, the contribution of assessment to student learning, the construction of relevant or connected experiences for students, the validity of the interpretations that teachers make and the bases for socially just assessment practices and outcomes. Central to an understanding of these conditions is awareness of the relationship between assessment, curriculum and pedagogy and the need for planning that can facilitate coherence between these message systems. Additionally, assessment comprehension for teachers should encompass teachers' knowledge of a variety of practical and written assessment techniques and the appropriate contexts and rationales for their use.

Connected with knowledge of the purposes of assessment is the requisite knowledge of information that teachers should provide students with following their engagement in assessment. For example, teachers need to understand the difference between justification for grades that they arrive at through the interpretation of the evidence presented by students and feedback on learning or performances. In particular, teachers should know the features of effective feedback and the relationship of feedback to future learning and assessment tasks.

This first element of assessment literacy will have a bearing on the fidelity to official curriculum and assessment expectations. In this regard, Brown

(2004) advised that, if systemic initiatives to improve teachers' assessment practices (literacies) are to be effective, they 'must deal with teachers' conceptions as much as they deal with declarative or procedural knowledge requirements' (p. 314). Brown's recommendations draw attention to the fact that teachers will have varying beliefs and understandings about assessment that will impact on how and why they engage in the process and the consequences of such engagement.

Assessment application

Assessment application has an obvious connection with assessment comprehension. It refers to the capacity of teachers to apply their knowledge of efficacious assessment practices in the secondary field of the classroom. In this regard it includes implementing assessment tasks and programmes that are consistent with these conditions as well as collecting and reproducing evidence of student learning to make valid and 'fit-for-purpose' interpretations of that evidence. Similarly, assessment application involves the provision of information to students concerning the task that supports the efficacy of assessment generally and informs the students specifically on the quality of the learning and performances and where attention could be prudently directed to enhance that learning and future performances.

Importantly, we argue that the planning and implementation of assessment needs to be realised in conjunction with curriculum planning and pedagogical practice. This is in contrast to traditional assessment practices in physical education that are more often than not an afterthought to the curriculum and pedagogy process and/or remain essentially disconnected from what is fundamentally taught or intended to be learnt.

Connected with a critical engagement in assessment (see element four) the assessment application of teachers will involve debriefing students as a class and individually, as required, following the assessment that they have participated in, to intervene on inappropriate or inaccurate student interpretations of the meanings associated with the assessment outcomes and to assist students in their productive use of this information. Moreover, such debriefing also allows teachers to ascertain the extent to which inappropriate interpretations are being made across a cohort to arrest concerns regarding consequential validity that can affect the general construct validity of the assessment processes being utilised.

Assessment interpretation

This element of assessment literacy refers to the sense that teachers make of the information they collect through the assessment tasks and programmes they implement and the implications that are derived and enacted as a consequence of those interpretations. Assessment interpretation has an obvious connection with validity, as validity refers to the soundness of interpretations, decisions and actions taken in relation to the information collected through assessment (Moss *et al.*, 2006). Knowledge about validity and valid practices are features of assessment comprehension. Assessment interpretation, in contrast, focuses on what teachers understand the information to mean in relation to the students' learning and progress, and their teaching practices, and what they actually do with the information. There are two key facets of this element that are of equal significance and that reflect the two primary purposes of assessment. First, interpretation involves teachers' utilisation of information to ascertain the learning progress of individual students and cohorts of students so that appropriate curricular and pedagogical adjustments can be made. This facet of interpretation will be evident in the adjustments that are made by teachers at the levels of the individual and the class cohort. The second facet of interpretation involves the referencing of the information collected on students through assessment against criteria and standards to determine levels of achievement or attainment.

Critical engagement with assessment

In the first instance, critical engagement with assessment requires one's awareness of the unavoidable and disproportionate distribution of power through the process of assessment. This element of assessment literacy promotes consideration of the contribution of assessment to the teacher's power in the field and its impact on the social dynamics of the classroom field. Moreover, it includes an understanding of the impact of teachers' assessment practices and their outcomes on individual students' perceptions of themselves. Fundamental to this consideration of assessment and power is the need to promote an understanding of power as dispersed and relational, and as inherently tied to the discourses and discursive relations that feature in and surround assessment texts and processes.

This element of assessment literacy is connected with assessment interpretation, as it affects teachers' understandings of the limits of interpretations that can be made about the information collected through assessment in physical education. It is evidenced through teachers' cautious treatment of this information and practical endeavours to communicate the limits of interpretations and dissuade inappropriate and unhelpful interpretations of the outcomes of assessment by students. In this regard an assessment-literate teacher recognises that assessment practices are never neutral, but rather are value laden in their construction (what to assess and what not to assess) and in their consequences (who receives what grade and on what basis the grades are assigned). Associated with this recognition, and underpinning the limits of acceptable interpretations, is an awareness of the numerous factors affecting students' responses and performance qualities in assessment tasks, and a realistic view of meritocratic aspirations of assessments.

Finally, an assessment-literate teacher is one who is aware of *their role in assessment* and in the establishment of the valuing systems operating within a field as a consequence of their assessment practices. Such awareness is describable as their reflexive capacities. Literacy involves making sense or meaning of the information. This meaning making is situated within, and mediated by, the values, beliefs and expectations of the person. As we mentioned in Chapter 5, reflexive capacities refer to the self-analysis of one's beliefs, values, history, etc. in the recognition that these aspects unavoidably influence one's perceptions of others and interactions with them. Focusing on the development of one's reflexive awareness in relation to assessment may aid teachers in their understanding of the influence they have over student achievement and opportunity to achieve and help them develop pedagogic and assessment practices that address the problematic consequences of such inferences.

Assessment literacy for physical education students

In general, the primary foci of assessment literacy for students are the same as for teachers. The obvious counterpoint is that, in the secondary field, students are subjected to assessment, while teachers are not. Nevertheless, there are some important similarities between the assessment literacy demands of teachers and students. First, students are required to make sense of assessment information that they receive from the teachers and to act on that information. Furthermore, students may be engaged as assessors themselves in instances of self-assessment and peer assessment that would be encouraged as part of an assessment-for-learning paradigm. In these instances the learning value and potential outcomes of such conduct will depend, in part, on students' understandings of assessment practice and the implementation of meaningful assessments.

It is important to recognise that students may develop different literacy capacities depending on their assessment histories with respect to the way they are taught to read or understand the information associated with their assessment, the amount and nature of the information they have received and the implications of different forms and sources of information for their futures, including their health, education and vocation. This means, of course, that, rather than focusing solely on providing students with better information about assessment and their engagement with it, initiatives to improve the literacy of students will also involve ascertaining and challenging prevailing and unhelpful understandings and beliefs about assessment, its purposes and its implications.

Assessment comprehension

To be able to effectively engage in assessment and demonstrate their learning in the way that is required by the teacher, physical education students need to understand what is expected of them, in terms of performance and learning representation. This requires fundamental literacy in terms of the capacity to engage with the texts through which assessment expectations are communicated, but also an understanding of how to respond to these expectations in a way that is consistent with the performance elements the teacher is requiring of them in the assessment task/process. In part this requires clarity from the teachers in terms of task expectations. Nevertheless, students need to be aware of the parameters of the assessment so that their responses are not limited by the generation of insufficient or irrelevant evidence.

We believe that it is important that students understand the features of good or efficacious assessment so that their expectations of teacher practice are increased and so that their own capacities to collect quality evidence of learning (either their own, or that of others) are optimised. Strengthening the capacities of students to collect meaningful evidence is an investment in both their learning independence and in their learning quality. This is a notable feature of learning-oriented assessment practices, which we argue in Chapter 7 is a necessary characteristic of efficacious assessment practices.

In order to benefit from assessment, students need to understand the information they should receive from the teacher concerning their assessment response. In particular they need to know and comprehend the difference between the information that teachers provide as justification for grading decisions and information that could be considered feedback and relevant to optimising future learning and performance.

Assessment application

Connected with assessment comprehension is the capacity of the students to enact the required assessment responses. To be clear, we are not asserting that the capacity to enact assessment is the same as, or equated with, achievement levels where those who achieve poorly have, by implication, poor assessment literacy. Rather our attention is directed towards the extent to which the responses of the students are indicative of what they know and can do without the compromising effect of misdirected efforts or misunderstood requirements.

The second aspect of assessment application is the students' own enactment of meaningful assessment practices for the purpose of collecting useful information on their own learning and the learning of their peers. In the earlier years of schooling, these capacities (the knowledge and application of assessment) are most likely to be optimally promoted and facilitated by teacher-produced self- and peer-assessment templates. As students develop greater capacity for learning independence it is necessary that they have the practical skills and the opportunities to implement those skills to ascertain their current learning in reference to defined objectives and make adjustments to their learning focus and approach as part of their own learning responsibility and accountability.

Similarly, students need to be able to source specific and meaningful feedback for themselves on their learning and their performance quality, and provide feedback to others that can be understood and can assist in another's learning progress. As we propose in Chapter 9, this element of application in the movement contexts of physical education will no doubt involve engagement with digital technologies that allow students to access evidence of their movement capacities, but also to manipulate and analyse that information for more cognitively oriented learning and assessment purposes.

Assessment interpretation

Students' assessment interpretation involves two elements. First, students need to be provided with the understanding of how teachers make sense of the information generated through assessment to arrive at grading decisions. This is particularly important in assessment contexts that utilise criteria and standards against which evidence of student learning is referenced. The second feature of students' assessment interpretation is their use of that information for future learning in physical education and future engagement in physical education assessment tasks.

The noted assessment theorist, Royce Sadler, argued that students need to be empowered in assessment contexts through their enhanced understanding of the basis for judgements of their learning and their performance quality. Specifically referring to judgements associated with the referencing of students' work against criteria and standards (rubrics), Sadler (1998) demanded that students be 'let in on the secret' of the meaning that teachers make of these criteria and standards and the relationship between the evidence of students' work and the statements. Notably, this requires teachers to make this relationship obvious to the students, but also requires that students have access to and understand the criteria and standards, and are able to interpret performance evidence against these statements for themselves. A useful strategy here, we propose, is to engage students in formative and individually oriented moderation of their performances in physical education so that there is a shared understanding of what the criteria and standards mean to teachers and students and what evidence is permissible for valid interpretations to be made. This will assist students' collection of their own evidence that teachers can use as part of their interpretations and grading processes.

The second key feature of assessment interpretation is students' use of the information associated with assessment for their ongoing learning in physical education. That is, students are able to use the feedback that they are provided with by teachers, or their peers, or that is collected through self-assessment, to optimise their learning in the psychomotor and cognitive domains of physical education and to inform their future engagement in assessment. In relation to this latter point, students' interpretation of assessment information is an important contributor to their ongoing development of assessment comprehension and application capacities.

Critical engagement with assessment

The notion of students' assessment literacy is concerned, in part, with questions of how students 'read' or consume the messages (information) that are communicated through assessment in physical education and the implications that this has for their perceptions of themselves and their ongoing engagement in a movement culture.

As with teachers' critical engagement with assessment, it is important that students are aware of the limitations of interpretations that can be made about assessment and learn to constrain their meaning making to these limits. Specifically and most helpfully for the students, recognition of the socially constructed basis of assessment development, enactment and outcomes should help students to understand that the outcomes of assessment should have a limited bearing on their futures. Students' critical engagement with assessment should also involve the development of their capacities to recognise the impact of key structuring values (and their sources) in the field contexts in which they are being assessed. Raising their awareness of these factors and the influences they can have on opportunities to learn and be assessed and on the interpretations of that information is an investment in their agency in the field and their opportunity to challenge discriminatory field practices and resultant structures.

Concluding comments

Enhancing the assessment literacy of students is a valuable way of empowering them in relation to a practice in which power is inherently disproportionate. Providing students with an understanding of efficacious assessment conditions raises their expectations of teachers' practices. Although we recognise the increased demands that this places on teachers we argue that students have an *entitlement* to assessment practices that are efficacious and should expect that inferences about their performances are valid. After all, it is the student who primarily bears the outcomes of the assessment (in terms of the grade and the implications of the grade). We believe that teachers should have a professional obligation to this, and that increasing students' assessment knowledge will result in a change in the focus and meaning of teacher accountability in schooling. By this we mean that teacher accountability can be refocused from performance scores that are consumed by a higher authority (or not at all) and directed to the students as the stakeholders who are most affected by the assessment practices of the teachers.

Of course, the risk of improving students' assessment literacy is that they may focus more on the process and outcomes of assessment than the learning that should be captured by it. That is, assessment literacy may promote performance or outcomes over learning. Arguably, this depends on the fundamental bases of what it means to be assessment literate. In this regard, we argue that an assessment-literate student is not so much one who knows about assessment and has high expectations of their own performance outcomes, but rather who understands how assessment may contribute to their own learning and who engages with the outcomes of assessment in a manner commensurate with that understanding. Similarly, an assessment-literate student will have a cautious and indeed critical perspective on grades and their meaning and will question both the outcomes and indeed the process itself. Thus, our emphasis is that assessment literacy is not dependent on, or a prerequisite for, high achievement, but rather refers to the capacities of teachers and students to engage with and utilise assessment practices and outcomes in a way that optimises learning possibilities.

Clearly the notion of assessment literacy in physical education is a new and undeveloped idea. We believe that the framework proposed in this chapter will provide a solid basis for ongoing discussion and conceptual work around assessment literacies for physical education teachers and students. Associated with such conceptual work and building on the previous assessment research in physical education is the need for empirical work focusing on teachers' existing assessment literacies. As we demonstrated in Chapter 5, research into physical education assessment highlighted the often trivial approaches to assessment by teachers (e.g. Hensley *et al.*, 1987; Matanin and Tannehill, 1994; Veal, 1988). What are not well documented are the understandings that students possess of assessment in general and assessment practices more specifically situated in the field of physical education. We encourage reflection, discussion, debate and challenge regarding our proposed elements of assessment literacy, including research initiatives that attend to the current literacies of teachers and students and ascertain the impact of enhancing the assessment literacies of these stakeholders on engagement and learning in physical education. While we have directed attention to the need for physical education teachers and students to both develop assessment literacy, we also recognise this as something that it is crucial for physical education teacher education (PETE) to engage with. We believe that the four elements of assessment literacy outlined in this chapter provide useful reference points for learning content and experiences of PETE students.

The next part of this book builds on the theoretical and conceptual foundations that have been laid thus far to more specifically examine the potential of assessment to benefit students and their learning in physical education. We have coined the term *assessment efficacy* to communicate the thought that assessment can be designed and implemented in such a way so as to elicit desired learning behaviours and effects as well as provide an information-collection mechanism for other purposes such as accountability. Such an approach foregrounds learning, but realises that assessment in institutional settings is necessary to serve other purposes. We argue that this goal depends upon a coherent and strategic alignment of the planning and implementation of curriculum, pedagogy and assessment.

Part III

Promoting assessment literacy in physical education

7 Aligning curriculum, pedagogy and assessment in physical education

Introduction

This part of the book introduces and focuses on assessment *efficacy*. In presenting a case for this concept to be a key point of reference for thinking about assessment and, more specifically, for debates and decisions regarding the design of assessment tasks, and the pedagogies of assessment, we also engage with the notion of *quality*. The chapter therefore begins with a discussion of efficacy and quality as they relate to assessment in physical education. Subsequent sections of the chapter then develop commentary in relation to some of the key issues and challenges arising from the conceptualisations of efficacy and quality that we present. Notably, these are premised on two things. First, the critical dynamics and interdependency of curriculum, pedagogy and assessment as message systems of physical education (see Chapter 2) and second, a foregrounding of Arnold's conceptualisation of learning 'in', 'through' and 'about' movement in considering the learnings that assessment in physical education should encompass and recognise. We deliberately refer to 'learnings' rather than 'learning' in order to make explicit the many forms and foci that a term such as 'learning in physical education' can be connected with, and to help keep to the fore the inherently contested nature of knowledge, learning and assessment in physical education.

The chapter thus reflects our view that debates about the learnings that assessment in physical education should address necessarily engage us (even if we do not acknowledge it) in debate about curriculum purposes as well as content, and requires us to consider what we might term 'the pedagogical dimension of assessment'. In many respects this chapter dispels clear distinctions between assessment, curriculum and pedagogy. Indeed, a central argument is that quality or efficacious assessment can only be realised in relation to quality curriculum and pedagogy and the clear alignment of these three message systems (Penney *et al.*, 2009). We therefore recognise curriculum and pedagogy as integral and highly influential in relation to our concerns with quality and efficacy in assessment in physical education. Accordingly, we pursue a deeper understanding of the ways in which the dynamics between assessment, curriculum and pedagogy can play out in physical education and, potentially, be influenced so as to advance quality and equity in physical education. In so doing, we explore the role that assessment may play as a catalyst for pedagogical change towards these ends.

We position Arnold's conceptualisation of learning 'in', 'through' and 'about' movement as central in considering the particular 'valued learnings' that assessment in physical education currently connects with, and arguably should seek to connect with. Thus, we emphasise the lack of neutrality of physical education curriculum, pedagogy and assessment and pursue the ways in which individually and collectively each of these connect with and thus accord value to, particular learnings. This reaffirms the significance that we attach to pedagogies of assessment and to exploring the learnings that curriculum frameworks and their associated assessment requirements or guidance, explicitly and implicitly, privilege or, in contrast, fail to acknowledge, or position as of marginal status.

Assessment efficacy and quality assessment

As we have noted elsewhere, a focus on assessment efficacy in physical education prompts consideration of the *desired outcomes* being sought from assessment, the effects of assessment and the factors that contribute to particular outcomes and effects (Hay and Penney, 2009). Efficacy refers to the capacity of something to produce a desired result or effect. It follows that assessment efficacy would refer to the *purposeful pursuit* of a *desired effect* of or though assessment. This requires, of course, that assessors consider why the assessment is being conducted and establish the intended consequences of that assessment. Similarly, it focuses attention on the deliberate alignment of task intent, construction, information generation, interpretations and consequences. The questioning that we allude to in taking this stance has multiple dimensions. This is reflected in our contention that 'assessment should be viewed as *a process through which learning can be promoted*' and, second, 'that the *satisfaction of this learning intent through the authentic, valid and socially just alignment of assessment, curriculum and pedagogy* is a basis for claims of efficacy' (ibid., p. 390, emphasis added). Assessment efficacy, from this perspective, is thus tied to a foregrounding of learning, and to the alignment of assessment, curriculum and pedagogy in ways that can be deemed authentic, valid and socially just, and an interest in the way assessment can be structured in such a manner as to promote particular learnings and learning behaviours.

Notions of assessment authenticity and validity are contestable and will inevitably reflect particular, and potentially very varied, views and expectations regarding the learnings and contexts of application which physical education should seek to address. Decisions on these matters are by no means neutral. Rather, they are inseparable from the social, cultural and epistemological views and understandings that underpin them. Hence, we also make explicit our simultaneous concern with social justice and stress that notions of quality in physical education are inherently linked to matters of equity, simply because all judgements about quality are, at the same time, judgements about the legitimacy and value of particular knowledge and ways of knowing in physical education. In turn they are, therefore, judgements that will privilege and advantage some students over others, by virtue of how students are differently positioned in terms of their relative abilities to access, develop and demonstrate valued knowledge in ways that are, similarly, deemed legitimate and are valued systemically in physical education and education. From this perspective, assessment efficacy is fundamentally concerned with 'the opportunities *all* students are given to engage in assessment, receive attention and recognition for demonstrations of performance, and *learn* as a consequence of their engagement in assessment' (Hay and Penney, 2009, p. 398, emphasis added). As we emphasise throughout this chapter, whether or not assessment addresses this concern requires consideration of assessment as a pedagogical process.

The centrality of learning in our conceptualisation of assessment efficacy and quality may appear to be stating something that is surely a given. Yet, as indicated in Chapter 1, the relationship between assessment and learning can be presented in varied ways and is reflected in the terminology of assessment 'of', 'in' or 'for' learning. In adopting the latter term, we stress that we are not merely concerned with 'the contribution of assessment to the learning process', but also, 'with the nature of learning being promoted and achieved' (Hay and Penney, 2009, p. 393) and, furthermore, *which* students are thereby supported or marginalised in physical education. We thus reaffirm that the alignment of assessment, curriculum and pedagogy is fundamental in how we are conceptualising quality in relation to assessment in physical education but, also, that none of this is neutral.

So, what learning should assessment in physical education be connecting with, supporting the development of and signalling as having worth?

Valued learning(s) – in, through and about physical education

The different knowledges and 'ways of knowing' that physical education can legitimately address and, furthermore, should seek to address, in and through assessment, are matters of long-standing debate in the field internationally and, particularly, in relation to senior secondary physical education (see, for example, Brown and Penney, 2011; Fitzclarence and Tinning, 1990; Green, 2005; Macdonald and Brooker, 1997a; Penney and Hay, 2008; Thorburn, 2007; Thorburn and Collins, 2003). It is in the senior secondary arena particularly that pressures to align the requirements of physical education with other established subjects that are deemed 'academic' have been most evident. This arena is also where course developers and teachers have grappled with whether and how learning and knowledge that is embodied and inherent in movement, and/or that can be demonstrated through movement performance, can be included in 'what is assessed' – particularly at the point of summative and external assessment in senior secondary schooling or examination physical education courses at the secondary level (such as GCSE[1] physical education courses in the UK). A point that has repeatedly been stressed in these debates (and that we have discussed in Part I of this book) is that 'what is assessed' at this point sends very powerful messages to teachers and students alike about 'what really counts'. By virtue of its inclusion in final summative assessment and/or external examinations, particular knowledge, expressed in a specific form and context, is very obviously accorded a higher value and status than that which is excluded.

Assessment, when equated (and reduced) in this way to a point in time or an isolated event, that is also openly associated with significant implications for the students concerned (in terms of future educational and/or career opportunities), represents and powerfully conveys a judgement call about the type and breadth of learning in physical education that is recognised by education systems as of worth. Yet, as anyone who has participated in course developments will be aware, the judgement call is simultaneously one that encompasses consideration of a number of matters, including the feasibility and perceived validity and reliability of particular assessments. Decisions about assessment requirements inevitably involve negotiation and compromise and, in recent years, they have arguably reflected tensions between forward-looking curricula (course designs) and a mix of perceived and actual limits of the sorts of assessment that can legitimately feature in physical education in 'high-stakes' educational settings (Penney *et al.*, 2011; Thorburn, 2007). Alternatively, debates and decisions made about assessment requirements for senior physical education courses internationally could be read as efforts to achieve a balance between parallel concerns for authenticity, feasibility, validity and reliability in assessment. In the discussion that follows, we pursue these issues further by turning to a framework that will be recognisable to many readers, and that is as pertinent to debates about curriculum and pedagogy in physical education as assessment: Arnold's (1979, 1988) dimensions of education 'in', 'through' and 'about' movement. While we retain a focus on physical education in the context of senior secondary schooling, we acknowledge and later expand upon the relevance and application of the issues to physical education in other phases of education.

As Brown and Penney (2011) recently acknowledged, Arnold's conceptualisation of these three dimensions of movement in relation to education and, more specifically, physical education, has informed a number of course/ syllabus developments in senior physical education internationally in recent years. While this is perhaps most explicit in Senior Physical Education in Queensland (QSA, 2010), the influence of Arnold's work can also be seen in the ways in which courses developed elsewhere – courses in Australia and in New Zealand, some of the A-level syllabuses in England and Wales and the Physical Education (Higher Still) in Scotland – have variously structured and presented course content for physical education at this level. Yet, as Brown and Penney (2011) also emphasised, while the language of 'in, through and about' is arguably now well established as part of the professional discourse of senior secondary physical education, there has also been clear variation in interpretations and application of Arnold's dimensions and increasing 'slippage' from Arnold's original language and intent. For example, while Arnold (1979) presented the three dimensions as 'Education *about* movement', 'Education *through* movement' and 'Education *in* movement' (p. 168, original emphasis), it is notable that the prime focus on *education* has not always been retained. The dimensions have invariably been rearticulated in relation to *learning* in, about and through *physical activity* and, as reflected in our own commentary, have often been reordered from Arnold's original presentation. To varying degrees, the dimensions have also underpinned conceptualisations and representations of 'informed' or 'intelligent' performance/performers in course documents and supporting texts (Kirk *et al.*, 2002, 2004).

We draw attention to these characteristics of recent developments for a number of reasons. First, how learning in physical education is conceptualised is in our view central to thinking about quality, equity and efficacy in assessment. Second, like Brown and Penney (2011), we see it as timely and potentially very valuable to bring people back to aspects of Arnold's original work as a means of renewing and extending debate about two matters that are of prime interest here: *What* learnings does, or should, assessment in physical education address or privilege?, and *How*? Third, in many instances, contemporary course or syllabus developments have brought to the fore the critical need for alignment of curriculum, pedagogy and assessment but, also, the clear challenges in achieving that. Once again, there are points in Arnold's original work that may assist in ongoing efforts to resolve some of the tensions noted in, for example, Thorburn and colleagues' work in Scotland (Thorburn, 2007; Thorburn and Collins, 2003).

Given our emphasis of the need to regard assessment as a process for facilitating learning, we discuss Arnold's dimensions with learning to the fore. As Brown and Penney (2011) indicated, each of the three dimensions can be seen as having a distinct epistemological orientation and focus:

- Learning *about* physical activity refers to a rational form of inquiry, where students directly acquire knowledge and understandings as a result of studying and participating in physical activity (e.g. examining the impact of gender stereotypes on participation in physical activity and planning psychological strategies for pre-match preparation). In the context of senior physical education, these understandings are typically applied in the interpretation, analysis, synthesis and evaluation of experiences in studying physical activity.
- Learning *through* physical activity refers to instrumental outcomes where students indirectly acquire understandings, capacities and attitudes as a result of studying and participating in physical activity (including, for example, increased physical fitness, aesthetic appreciation of a performance, continued participation in a physical activity).
- Learning *in* physical activity refers to experiential outcomes, where students directly acquire knowledge, understandings and skills as a

result of thoughtful participation in physical activity (e.g. applying tactics and strategies in a game, appraising the physical capacities and requirements of an activity).

(Brown and Penney, 2011)

The dimensions articulated in relation to learning in this way provide a useful frame for critical review of what learning, curriculum, pedagogy and assessment individually and collectively encompass, privilege or marginalise. We can question not only whether the three dimensions are equally reflected in physical education curriculum, pedagogy and assessment (and indeed, whether equal representation of each should be sought) but also, and perhaps more importantly, whether physical education curriculum, pedagogy and assessment has succeeded in capturing the critical inter-connectedness of the three dimensions that Arnold (1979) highlighted. Arnold described the dimensions as 'conceptually discrete but functionally related. Each dimension is not exclusive of the others, but overlaps and merges into them' (Arnold, 1979, p. 177). The inter-connectedness, should, we contend, be fundamental to thinking about the structure and content of physical education curriculum, pedagogy and assessment. With others (Thorburn, 2007), we recognise the development of formal, summative assessment in senior physical education as the point at which the inter-connectedness of Arnold's dimensions will, from a pedagogical perspective, either be clearly reaffirmed, or effectively be lost. In turn, we see the authenticity of teaching and learning in physical education as clearly strengthened, or openly compromised. This reflects our view that quality assessment tasks should provide students with opportunities to demonstrate the valued learnings defined by the curriculum 'in' and 'about' movement, without compromising the beneficial affective effects that may be realised 'through' movement.

Before exploring these issues further, it would be remiss to gloss over a further matter of terminology pertinent to our discussion. Specifically, we highlight that, while Brown and Penney (2011) chose to consider learning about, through and in *physical activity*, here we revert to Arnold's original focus on *movement*. In so doing, we recall Arnold's (1979) own emphasis of 'richness and diversity' and thus seek to maintain breadth in relation to the forms of movement that physical education curricula can encompass and, therefore, that assessment should also connect with.

Focusing on the three dimensions, we now consider whether and to what extent assessment tasks in physical education typically promote learning reflected in each dimension and, also, represented by the three collectively. We thus prompt critical reflection about whether assessment tasks capture the functional relationship between the dimensions that Arnold emphasised. Furthermore, we are interested in *how* particular learning connections are either made or marginalised by virtue of task specifications, the learning contexts chosen or prescribed for assessment tasks and what we refer to as the pedagogies of assessment. As indicated above, the latter term consciously signals a blurring of boundaries between pedagogy and assessment, and may go some way towards countering the tendency for talk of 'tasks' to again constrain thinking about assessment in physical education to particular times or events.

Assessment and learning 'about' movement

As indicated above, Arnold (1979) identified education 'about' movement as centring on bodies of (disciplinary) knowledge that are incorporated in human movement 'as a subject to be studied' (p. 169, emphasis removed), and that are invariably explicit as content knowledge in examination physical education courses. Arnold's comments on the focus and significance of the knowledge that is central to this dimension are pertinent to consider in relation to assessment:

> It is largely of the propositional kind and is capable of being presented in a discursive way. It is public and objective, in principle sharable, and therefore communicable. It has the merit of providing a theoretical background of understanding which helps make coherent and meaningful that which is performed. In this respect, knowing 'about' movement can act as an analytical as well as a critical and evaluative aspect of movement education.
>
> (Arnold, 1979, p. 170)

As many readers will recognise, this is precisely how learning 'about' movement features in many senior secondary or other examinable physical education syllabuses and curricula. Variously, knowledge and concepts associated with, for example, physiology, biomechanics, psychology or sociology are engaged with in order to inform and enhance analysis, evaluation and/or critical reflection. In thinking about assessment tasks that focus on these bodies of knowledge and that purportedly also, therefore, seek to address learning 'about' movement, we prompt critical reflection about the nature and orientation of tasks, particularly in relation to prospective ongoing learning and application of knowledge. While many assessment tasks may well go beyond knowledge or factual 'recall' and engage students in analysis or evaluation of patterns of movement, participation trends and specific incidents or events, in many instances, tasks have historically also been seemingly constrained by virtue of the recognition and/or expectation that the knowledge central to learning about movement 'is capable of being presented in a discursive way' (Arnold, 1979, p. 170). In examination contexts particularly, 'written' has invariably been substituted for 'discursive', with short-answer and/or extended-response format questions, and some of these requiring or allowing for graphical, diagrammatic or some other visual text representation of knowledge. As we discuss further in Chapter 9, new technologies are clearly extending possibilities in relation to the types and format of assessment tasks that are deemed both feasible and sufficiently rigorous for externally examined assessment in particular.

'School-based' or 'internal' assessment tasks have a far longer history of challenging the dominance of written response in 'high-stakes' assessment in physical education. In enabling, for example, oral reflective commentaries linked to a video clip of a performance, or embedded video-analysis using specialist software packages, tasks have arguably given greater attention to both application of knowledge and the connectedness of Arnold's dimensions. Yet, in contemplating tasks that focus on learning 'about', we can surely question the extent to which assessment in physical education has heeded Arnold's (1979) point that, 'Apart from studying movement as a theoretical body of knowledge that is of interest in its own right, *it can be studied in order to apply it to practical situations*' (p. 169, our emphasis) and, furthermore, that such application is invariably the prime motivation for students, and a prominent learning objective of curricula. Thus, we are prompted to question whether assessment tasks in senior secondary and other examination physical education courses adequately adopt an 'assessment for learning' and, more specifically, 'assessment for applied learning' orientation and, in parallel, consider whether devoting greater attention to the inter-connectivity of Arnold's three dimensions is a key means of enhancing assessment efficacy in this regard. At the same time, it is pertinent to also reflect on the ways in which assessment tasks in non-examinable physical education and, thus, the majority of primary and secondary physical education curricula, address learning 'about' movement. While it is neither feasible nor appropriate here to move into a debate about the respective scope of Kindergarten to Year 10 (K–10) curricula and examination courses in physical education, we are acutely aware that in posing questions of assessment we are inevitably and simultaneously raising issues about curriculum and pedagogy. Although to some extent that is an intention in this text, we wish to retain a clear focus on assessment. Thus, in this instance, we suggest that amidst an ongoing situation in many countries of a notable disjuncture in the scope, demands and expectations for teaching and learning in physical education in non-examination as compared to examination contexts, there are perhaps two points to raise, pertinent to our discussion here. From one standpoint, a reaction from many students, teachers or other stakeholders contemplating assessment in what we might term 'core' (i.e. non-examination) physical education curricula, might well be that the sort of knowledge foregrounded in Arnold's notion of education 'about' movement, is quite consciously acknowledged as either not a focus of or for assessment, or as a peripheral aspect of assessment in 'core' physical education. An alternative perspective is that, while not always as explicit as it could or even should be, knowledge directly relevant to this dimension is often inherent in tasks that are integral to assessment in many core physical education curriculum contexts. In saying this, we reaffirm the legitimacy of blurred boundaries – between learning experiences and assessment tasks, and between pedagogy and assessment. Thinking, then, about what many teachers might refer to as 'ongoing' assessment, integral to their lesson-by-lesson teaching activities are instances whereby learning 'about' movement is clearly addressed. Furthermore, students are called upon to demonstrate it in interactions with teachers and/or peers (for example in taking on a coaching task in a lesson adopting a Sport Education (Siedentop, 1994) approach, and in their embodied actions and movement responses. In this sense, application of learning 'about' movement is acknowledged as integral to and embodied in 'performance' in physical activity and sporting contexts, such that a 'performance task' is deemed capable of engaging with this learning from an assessment standpoint. In Chapter 9 we explore these issues further, drawing on contemporary developments and recent research in senior secondary physical education.

Assessment and learning 'in' movement

While education and learning 'about' movement is characterised as holding the potential to be separated pedagogically from embodied movement and learning, Arnold (1979) distinguished education 'in' movement as concerned with 'the values that are an inherent part of the activities themselves' (p. 176). This dimension thus privileges the embodied activities that feature in physical education curricula by virtue that 'they are "body-orientated", culturally significant and synnoetically meaningful' (p. 178). Arnold explained that addressing learning 'in' movement thus requires experiences that enable the intrinsic worth of movement to be realised such that its inherent values will be made manifest. At this point we might justifiably question how assessment can directly and furthermore, authentically, engage with intrinsic worth and values. In part, Arnold assists us in a response, with his parallel emphasis that this dimension cannot be conceived of in isolation:

> The notion of education 'in' movement then is not a self-contained or distinct entity. Although it emphasizes the process of moving it relates to and draws upon the other dimensions at different times and in varying degrees according to the situation in hand.
>
> (1979, p. 178)

Yet, while engaging with these linkages, we should not overlook that this dimension accords value to the personal experience and act of 'being' and 'moving', with the understanding that 'Movement in meeting its own internal rules, standards and traditions *is in and of itself educative*' (Arnold, 1979, p. 178, our emphasis). From an assessment viewpoint, this requires us to foreground experiential, embodied learning, and to not only design tasks that retain this emphasis, but also ensure that the same emphasis carries through to assessment criteria and judgements. *What* assessment tasks require students to do, and *how*, are both clearly critical and inter-related in seeking to foreground learning 'in' movement. By necessity, the learning task and evidence of learning will be self-oriented and embodied: inherent in and inseparable from performance. To go beyond this is to extend assessment to encompass elements of the 'functional relationship' with the other dimensions. While we want to avoid implying that to do this is problematic (since we are interested in pursuing greater representation of the inter-connectedness of the dimensions in assessment), the balancing of clear engagement with any single dimension while, simultaneously, representing the dynamic, is challenging and we do not pretend to have definitive answers to this or indeed many of the issues we raise. Rather, we share with others a desire to explore the limits of understanding and thinking about assessment in physical education. In relation to the challenges specifically associated with connecting with learning 'in' movement, as Thorburn (2007) has discussed, historically, various senior secondary course developments have sought to foreground personal experience in and of movement or physical activity and to therefore also orientate curriculum, pedagogy and assessment towards 'personalised learning'. Thorburn (2007) recognised the prospective merits of adopting a phenomenological approach as a means of trying to enhance the 'conceptual coherence' of contemporary senior secondary physical education courses, with tasks that, therefore, focus directly on the lived experience of participation, performance and movement. Thorburn (2007) observed that 'greater use of discussion records, student diaries and log-books suggest themselves as worthy of critical consideration for teaching, learning and assessment purposes' (p. 180). We similarly advocate for assessment to be considered 'pedagogically' and, thus, for these and other possibilities to be explored in relation to the sorts of teaching and learning programmes and experiences that curricula enable and/ or encourage teachers to develop. As we discuss further in Chapter 9, new technologies clearly extend the ways in which we can think about both assessment tasks and assessment methods, or tools such as diaries or journals, and may enable learning 'in' movement to be embedded more authentically in assessment.

Assessment and learning 'through' movement

As Arnold (1979) himself acknowledged, education 'through' movement is, in many respects, the dimension that aligns most directly with commonly held understandings of 'physical education' as a school subject. He explained that this dimension entails 'that culture based family of activities and processes – games, dance, gymnastics, athletics, swimming, outdoor pursuits, etc' being employed 'as a means through which the teacher can help effect desired outcomes, regardless of whether or not those activities have intrinsic worth of their own' (p. 171). From this perspective, the curriculum is unashamedly instrumental in its orientation and, as Arnold (1979) recognised, the scope of the instrumental outcomes that physical education has been linked with is diverse, spanning physical health benefits, moral aspects of education, and social and emotional development. Perhaps somewhat contentiously, we suggest that, amidst an ongoing tendency for many and varied claims to be made about what is (or can be) achieved as a consequence of students' participation in physical education, assessment can serve a somewhat cautionary function. In essence we bring attention back to a need for alignment between curriculum purposes, pedagogy and assessment and, in this instance, therefore see a need for clarity in relation to the instrumental outcomes that any curriculum is explicitly seeking to engage with – and for that to then be reflected in assessment tasks. In saying this we are not implying that these outcomes and, thus, this dimension should be the prime driver of assessment but, rather, that tasks should seek to engage with (particular) learning 'through' movement as one of three inter-related dimensions of learning. Amidst ongoing clear pressures internationally for physical education to justify its curriculum position and ongoing resourcing in instrumental ways, we urge the balance and dynamic between learning 'about', 'in' and 'through' to be at the fore of thinking about assessment particularly. The section that follows therefore focuses on the issues and implications associated with this approach. In so doing, it directs attention to 'pedagogies of assessment'.

Learning 'about', 'in' and 'through' movement: pursuing the dynamic in and through assessment

In returning to view the three dimensions collectively and specifically, we do so with assessment in mind and we recall Arnold's (1979) emphasis that the dimensions are 'functionally related', such that the concept of movement that they convey is 'a mutually reinforcing and inter-dependent one' (p. 177). We contend that *learning* 'about', 'in' and 'through' needs to therefore be similarly conceived of, and that adopting and expressing this conception is a necessary step in addressing assessment efficacy in physical education. As indicated in opening sections of this chapter, *authenticity, quality* and *equity* are integral to our view of assessment efficacy. The inter-related, holistic conceptualisation of learning that derives from Arnold's three-dimensional presentation of movement and education is a foundation from which we can perhaps better engage with and advance assessment efficacy in physical education. As Hay (2006) has previously highlighted, to address authenticity, assessment in physical education needs to be 'based in movement and capture the cognitive and psychomotor processes involved in the competent performance of physical activities' (p. 317). Assessment tasks *and pedagogy* are both key to achieving this and to therefore bringing to the fore 'the interrelatedness of knowledge, process (cognitive and motor), skills and the affective domain' (ibid., p. 317). From this perspective, designing assessment tasks necessarily involves consideration of the sort of pedagogies that will provide students with the requisite skills and knowledges to successfully engage with the tasks. Furthermore, it prompts us to then consider how particular types and modes of assessment task can act as a catalyst for, or barrier to, pedagogical change in physical education.

Concluding comments

Talk of change is always contentious and, understandably, can give rise to the challenge, 'Why do we need to talk of change?' In response, we routinely ask if current assessment practices can claim to meet the conditions we have identified as necessary for assessment efficacy: Is assessment clearly and consistently oriented towards the process of learning, and are assessment, curriculum and pedagogy aligned in ways that can be deemed authentic, valid and socially just? In centring much of our discussion on Arnold's (1979) three dimensions, our intention has been to generate questions about the extent to which and ways in which current assessment tasks, contexts and processes variously enable connections with the different knowledges that each dimension encompasses – or alternatively, limit or preclude particular connections. Our emphasis is that answers to these questions have implications for not only *what* learning assessment in physical education will serve to legitimate and signal as valued but, simultaneously, what will be deemed legitimate ways in which to learn and to demonstrate learning in physical education and, finally, therefore, *who* feels able to learn and achieve in physical education. For us, assessment viewed as inherently tied to curriculum and pedagogy and, more specifically, the concept of assessment efficacy, presents an invaluable avenue via which to engage with these long-standing and ongoing issues for physical education.

Building on our claims for assessment that is efficacious and necessarily oriented towards movement, our next chapter seeks to contribute to discussions about assessment that is learning-oriented in physical education by reconceptualising what might be understood as 'assessment for learning' in physical education and by proposing consideration of 'lifelong' and 'lifewide' learning and assessment.

8 Reconceptualising assessment for learning in physical education

Introduction

This chapter seeks to further develop appreciation of the contribution that assessment can make to student learning. The notion of assessment *for learning* is therefore once again foregrounded and, specifically, linked with an endeavour to promote the contemporary relevance and connectedness of assessment and learning in physical education with the lives and experiences of young people. In addressing relevance and connectedness, much of our discussion also relates to a concern to enhance authenticity in assessment in physical education. In parallel, and in line with our interest in assessment efficacy (see Chapter 7), we emphasise the need to always consider relevance, connectedness and authenticity from the perspective of each and every individual student. Inevitably, such statements can be deemed idealistic and are in danger of being dismissed as too far removed from pedagogical realities to justify engagement. Yet, we retain the stance that valuing individual students' learning needs, interests, personal life circumstances and values is fundamental to equity in physical education and, more particularly, assessment in physical education.

This chapter thus poses critical questions of assessment in relation to matters such as: Whose 'worlds and lives beyond the classroom' is assessment in physical education relating to and connecting with? How, variously, does the content, context and the pedagogy of assessment impact upon this prospective connection? In exploring these and other issues we take two tacks initially. First, we focus on the contribution of assessment in physical education to lifelong learning. We then turn attention to the notion of 'lifewide' learning, a concept adopted from West (2004) and, arguably, highly pertinent yet underdeveloped in physical education curriculum debates – and, therefore, also debates about pedagogy and assessment! In addressing assessment from both lifelong and lifewide perspectives, we explore assessment design, enactment and, therefore, the learning experience and prospective value of assessment from a student's standpoint, with authenticity, equity and efficacy in mind. The final section of our discussion reflects that, ultimately, we cannot justifiably consider lifelong and lifewide learning as separate or distinct entities. We therefore direct attention to the challenge of developing assessment tasks and practices that embrace both of these concerns simultaneously. In so doing, we further explore assessment in physical education in relation to the notion of 'real world challenges' and reaffirm a case for assessment tasks and pedagogy to promote the integration of the cognitive, psychomotor and affective domains of learning. We argue that the ways and contexts in which this integration is pursued via assessment are fundamental in relation to concerns for assessment to be seen as aligning with students' 'real worlds' now and in the future.

Assessment for lifelong learning

Necessarily, before directing attention specifically to assessment matters, we need to say something about the concept of lifelong learning in general and in relation to physical education in particular. Following others (Penney and Jess, 2004), we recognise that varied conceptualisations of lifelong learning will have a direct bearing upon its prospective expression in and through physical education curriculum, pedagogy and assessment. As Penney and Jess (2004) indicated, amidst curriculum debates or pronouncements in physical education that seek political and public support from a lifelong perspective, there is clear potential for attention to centre on a number of issues that, whilst important, may overshadow consideration of lifelong *learning*. Sustained participation in physical activity (including sport), various health conditions, aspects of well-being and lifestyle behaviours all fall into this category. The primacy of discourses of physical activity, sport and health amidst discussion of lifelong learning in physical education is understandable, given their prominence relative to educational discourses in wider curriculum debates (Evans, 2004). Yet, such debates can also result in a reductionist view of lifelong learning, by focusing exclusively on the prospective contexts of application of learning, rather than an ongoing process of learning in and through physical education that, itself, is no longer conceived of as bounded by school years or gates (Penney and Jess, 2004). We therefore endeavour to foreground the notion of a learning process that extends beyond formal education in spatial and temporal terms, by retaining a focus on assessment *for learning*. We also emphasise that the expression of lifelong learning in physical education requires that curriculum, pedagogy and assessment are all directed towards an ongoing process of learning.

The notion of *process* has featured consistently in descriptions of lifelong learning. For example, the Lifelong Learning Foundation talked of 'an interconnected process of cumulative learning, extending from the "cradle-to-grave" and having the learner at the heart of the process' (Brookes, 2004, p. vi). The European Lifelong Learning Initiative identified the process with notions of empowerment *to* learn and *through* learning, and as involving both acquisition and application:

> Lifelong learning is a continuously supportive process which stimulates and empowers individuals to acquire all the knowledge, values, skills and

understanding they will require throughout their lifetimes and to apply them with confidence, creativity and enjoyment in all roles, circumstances, and environments.

(European Lifelong Learning Initiative, cited in Watson, 2003, p. 3)

Definitions such as this are a valuable reference point for critical reflection on the contribution of assessment in physical education to lifelong learning and, as indicated above, reaffirm the need for an inter-connected vision of curriculum, pedagogy and assessment. Viewing lifelong learning as a process that should be characterised by feelings of competence, ability and enjoyment challenges us to foreground those same feelings when we think about assessment in physical education. Without this orientation, it is hard to envisage that assessment will play its part in encouraging the ongoing acquisition of skills, knowledge and understandings, or their application in new contexts. Thus, we are prompted to ask, for example, whether students would regard current assessment in physical education as supportive, enabling and empowering? And, perhaps particularly, how those students who would typically be deemed by both teachers and their peers as 'low ability' would see assessment. Similarly, we can question the extent to which either the content (knowledge, skills and understandings) being addressed by assessment tasks, or the contexts and ways in which students are required to demonstrate particular knowledge, skills and understanding, are oriented towards prospective future application. Are our current assessment tasks actively promoting an understanding of the potential life relevance and lifelong application of the skills, knowledge and understandings that are addressed in and through physical education? And, importantly, what will it take to enhance the connection between assessment and lifelong learning in physical education?

Inevitably, in posing questions such as these we are engaging with what might well be deemed 'curriculum' (rather than assessment) matters, concerning what skills, knowledge and understandings associated with physical education can be regarded as having lifelong relevance. Penney and Jess's (2004) commentary pointed to a need for broader and longer-term thinking about 'physically active lives' in order to identify the range of skills, knowledge and understandings that, arguably, physical education should be addressing from a 'lifelong' perspective. Penney and Jess (2004) thus introduced the notion of a curriculum centring on 'functional', 'recreational', 'health-related' and 'performance-related' physical activity, and addressing skills, knowledge and understandings pertinent to each. Their proposals drew attention to areas of knowledge, skills and understandings that would not typically feature in many physical education (or HPE) curricula currently and challenged the arguably narrow orientation (and thus limited lifelong relevance) of sport- and/or performance-oriented curricula. Other curriculum debates and developments have similarly pointed to the limitations inherent in the multi-activity curriculum model, and more so when the application of skills, knowledge and understandings beyond physical education is considered. For example, an expanded range of skills, knowledge and under-standings, relating directly to a concern for curricula to encourage and enable students to participate in roles other than 'performer' in sporting contexts, and to become 'critical consumers of sport', has been central to the Sport Education model (Siedentop, 1994) and the extensive research and literature associated with it internationally (see, for example, Wallhead and O'Sullivan, 2005; Hastie, 2012). Similarly, work associated with the Teaching Games for Understanding (TGfU) model (Thorpe *et al.*, 1986) has addressed the transfer of skills, knowledge and understanding across various sports and physical activities. This model can thus be seen as supporting breadth in terms of application of learning and prospectively more sustained exploration and application of learning. Yet, research addressing the application, relevance and further development *post-school* of skills, knowledge and understandings gained 'in, about and through' physical education via Sport Education, TGfU or other models remains lacking. Nevertheless, these models can be seen as providing some important insights and generating issues pertinent to our interest in assessment 'for lifelong learning'.

In Sport Education literature, the potential for assessment tasks associated with a number of roles (e.g. coach, captain, journalist) to be developed that openly require students to demonstrate skills, knowledge and understandings that would enable and empower them to take on these roles beyond school, is clear (Kinchin, 2001; Penney *et al.*, 2005; Taggart *et al.*, 1995; Wallhead and O'Sullivan, 2005). This work also highlights, however, that, with interests in authenticity and prospective future acquisition and application of learning in mind, the pedagogy of assessment – relating to *how and when* assessment tasks are enacted, *who* is involved in judgement processes, and *the criteria* applied in that process – are all arguably as important as the particular skills and knowledge encompassed in a task. Indeed, all these aspects of assessment will impact on the extent to which participation in an assessment task pro-motes the desire, competence and confidence to further explore and apply learning post a season of Sport Education and post-school, as a volunteer coach, manager, club captain, reporter, secretary or official. For assessment tasks and experiences in physical education to have elements of both 'real world' and 'lifelong' relevance, assessment tasks will necessarily blur with and be integral to learning experiences. Assessment of, for example, the skills, knowledge and understanding associated with live sport commentary, can thus be envisaged as a progressive learning and assessment task, involving a number of scaffolded steps and experiences. These might include:

• Listening to and sharing deconstruction of a sport commentary, to identify key characteristics of the commentary, relating to content and style, and to engage with critique of skill execution, decision making, other strategic aspects of performance or incidents that raise issues of fair play. Different students within a group or team could be assigned responsibility to focus on particular aspects of the commentary. A group task in-class could generate an analysis framework for students to use with other extracts of commentary, or to use in then looking at other forms of sport reporting, such as match reports in newspapers.

- Using the group task in-class as the basis for an individual task beyond class, enabling students to select a commentary or report from a sport of their choice for analysis and, thus, focus on a context with personal relevance. Peer assessment within Sport Education teams could enhance the shared learning arising from this assessment task.

- Developing a commentary from a pre-recorded section of play, or producing a written match report for a newspaper, from a recorded game in one of their Sport Education lessons. This may again be a peer-learning/-assessment task, with students working in pairs to review the play, discuss key points and breaks that will structure their commentary or report, share in a 'trial' at the task and then potentially peer assess each others' 'final product' using criteria discussed and developed amongst each Sport Education team and negotiated with the teacher.

- Undertaking and recording a live commentary for a section of a competition within the Sport Education season, or producing a written match report for 'instant publication' immediately after the competition. For either task students could undertake self-assessment using the team's agreed criteria and share the self-assessment with a peer to come up with an agreed final assessment result for this part of the task.

At each stage, assessment is designed to support and extend learning, through extending task demands, but also through the pedagogy of the task. Choices within the task are provided to enhance the extent to which individual learning interests, styles and abilities can be addressed. Finally, the learning that is potentially advanced through the task – most notably, students' knowledge and understanding of aspects of their own performance and ways to potentially improve this, can be seen as extending beyond the learning that is the focus of assessment judgements.

In relation to TGfU, Mitchell *et al.*'s (2006) work stands out as promoting alignment of curriculum, pedagogy and assessment specifically through the application of the Games Performance Assessment Instrument (GPAI). The instrument makes explicit skills, knowledge and understandings that are identified as transferable across game contexts, and elements of the GPAI (such as 'base', decision making or 'support') can provide a focus for learning and assessment tasks, spanning familiar and new activity contexts or situations. With a focus on future extension and application of learning via a role other than participant/performer, a peer coaching task could be designed based on selected elements of the GPAI. A progressive design can again serve to scaffold learning, emphasise assessment for learning and enable students to make a number of connections to various roles and responsibilities that they might engage with post-school. Students could, for example, be challenged to:

- Undertake a video-review of a section of play from a class game, focusing on one or multiple elements of GPAI. This could be a peer or group task with, e.g. different pairs focusing on different elements or the performance of particular players. Peer assessment of performance could thereby be undertaken in a way that also requires students to develop and demonstrate game understanding.
- Develop and implement a coached practice session that is informed by the analysis and designed to enhance performance relating to a specific element of GPAI. This could be a task undertaken by pairs of students sharing the coaching role and running the session for their team/group. Peer assessment, focusing on the design of the practice and the coaching skills demonstrated, could then be undertaken by the rest of the team.
- Challenge individual students adopting the role of coach to make 'live' judgements about game performance and provide key feedback to a team in a 'timeout' or quarter-/half-time break coaching 'window'. Self-reflection via a journal entry could accompany teacher assessment for this part of the task.

As with the preceding task, the final part of the assessment is designed to relate as directly as possible to 'real life' responsibilities and challenges that students might take up in their lives post-school and to encourage them to do just that.

Our discussion thus far reflects that we want to emphasise the 'lifelong' connections that assessment in physical education can facilitate, and reaffirm the key role that assessment in physical education can potentially play in encouraging and enabling students' ongoing learning. At the same time, we recognise that viewing students' prospective further development and application of learning from a solely temporal (post-school years) perspective has limitations. The section that follows therefore takes a more spatial perspective. It focuses on prospective links between learning and assessment in physical education, and learning occurring 'in parallel' to formal education, in varied contexts, amidst students' lives beyond the school gates.

Assessment for lifewide learning

'Lifewide' learning is a term that we adopt from West (2004) and that, somewhat surprisingly, has received relatively little attention in physical education literature. Surprising, that is, because traditionally physical education has made much of links between physical education curriculum experiences, co- or extra-curricular learning and students' application and further development of that learning in their lives beyond schools, particularly in organised junior sport and more informal physical activity. The concept of lifewide learning has some important commonalities with lifelong learning as we have articulated it above. Specifically, lifewide learning similarly promotes a view of learning as not bounded by institutional structures or settings and acknowledges that learning occurs in many different ways, in various settings throughout one's life. Technological developments in recent decades have clearly enhanced appreciation of the need for formal education to recognise and better connect with learning opportunities that, on a day-to-day basis, children encounter. This aligns with Bentley's (1998) vision of the learner as 'an intelligent agent with the potential to learn from any and all of her encounters with the world around her' (p. 1), and as Hargreaves (2004) emphasised, prompts educationalists to conceive of learning and, more specifically, their role in facilitating learning, as part of a process that extends beyond the formal curriculum and beyond schools. Teachers, from this perspective, are just one of many pedagogues, and schools are one site within a network of learning.

Penney (2008, p. 40) has previously acknowledged that:

> How to develop curriculum, courses and pedagogies that recognize, effectively utilize and help to enhance any individual student's learning networks and resources – and that, furthermore, draw upon and draw in the sporting communities, family and friendship groups that they may be a part of – is by no means a question with any simple answers.

We reaffirm that, nevertheless, developing curriculum, pedagogies and, furthermore, assessment in ways that foreground the notion of lifewide education remains a key agenda for physical education. In stating this we are very aware that a response might well be that, historically, many physical education teachers, departments and schools have sought precisely these learning connections and that, furthermore, they continue to do so. Yet, while the discourse of 'physical education and school sport' (PESS) and a number of policy contexts internationally point to policy and pedagogical boundaries between physical education, physical activity and sport being increasingly blurred (see Penney, 2011; Petrie and lisahunter, 2011), we contend that 'blurring' does not necessarily equate to coherency in the learning opportunities being provided within and beyond the school. Furthermore, as Flintoff's (2008) work in the UK highlights, we cannot assume that policy developments directed towards new or enhanced partnerships will translate into quality and equitable learning connections for all students. In focusing specifically on assessment, we hope to draw attention to considerable and arguably underdeveloped potential for lifewide learning to be facilitated in and through physical education.

As indicated throughout this text, we are promoting a view of assessment as necessarily linked to pedagogical and curriculum considerations but, also, as a potential catalyst for pedagogical and curriculum change. That potential will be evident in the discussion that follows, in which we consider the types of assessment task that will promote and require students to draw on learning experiences and contexts beyond the school and also encourage and enable them to extend their learning outside school. Essentially, we are seeking tasks and pedagogies that make explicit and actively enhance the 'dynamic' between learning in physical education and learning occurring in multiple contexts, including club, community and family-based sport and physical activity. In parallel, we emphasise that tasks need to promote connections between teachers and the other pedagogues who contribute to students' learning, including sport leaders and coaches in the community, parents, siblings and friends, and will require enhanced communication and collaboration between these various pedagogues. Our discussion clearly raises the issue of the extent to which assessment should be bounded by schools as institutions or, more specifically, by the formal curriculum. Our stance is that, if supporting and enhancing lifewide learning is identified as a curriculum and pedagogical goal (for education as a whole and physical education specifically), that goal should then be reflected in the sorts of assessment tasks that students are challenged to undertake, the contexts those tasks require or enable them to utilise, and who is involved pedagogically in supporting 'assessment for lifewide learning'.

The notion of an enhanced 'dynamic' across and between the various sites of learning that feature in students' lives provides a valuable steer for thinking about both assessment task design and pedagogy. Contexts such as junior club or community sport, and participation in activities with family or friends, are acknowledged as providing experiences and insights that students should routinely be encouraged to *draw upon and relate to* in assessment tasks in physical education. Above we discussed the GPAI and highlighted it as a framework for assessment that promotes extended learning and application across different activities within physical education. The elements incorporated in the GPAI clearly lend themselves to exploration in varied contexts, which can include out-of-school organised or informal sport participation, and thereby enable students to potentially select element(s) most applicable to their personal interests and explore those in openly authentic settings. As one component of an integrated lifewide assessment task, students could, for example, undertake self- and/or peer assessment using the GPAI in an out-of-school context of their choice. The results of such a task could be used within physical education curriculum setting for students to work on designing practice activities with peers that reflect the key areas for development identified through their analyses. Undertaking this part of the task in groups or teams would facilitate breadth in learning, through the sharing of experiences and application of learning in a number of activity contexts that students are variously involved in outside school. Looking more directly at the application and extension of learning *from* a physical education curriculum context *to* an out-of-school context, having worked on a particular aspect of performance, or specific skill development, in curriculum time, assessment may centre on students' abilities to apply their learning in a participation context beyond the curriculum or outside school.

In considering the pragmatic aspects of such suggestions, pedagogical links and relations come to the fore. For these or any similar suggestions for assessment to 'cross boundaries' and promote learning connections, there is a clear need for greater collaboration and communication between teachers and 'other pedagogues' who share an interest in and desire to support a student's learning. The perspectives that peers (friends or siblings) and other adults (including parents and community or club sport leaders and coaches) can potentially bring to assessment tasks represent a significant pedagogical resource. While many teachers may feel understandably hesitant about developing tasks that require involvement of others in the assessment process, we contend that such involvement, and the communication that it entails, is fundamental if assessment in physical education is to develop a lifewide learning perspective. Essentially, we are advocating both tasks and pedagogies that reflect the complexities of learning that are integral to students' daily lives and that seek to better support students in making sense of that complexity and maximising opportunities to learn within and beyond schools. We openly acknowledge that not every attempt to develop such links will go smoothly, but believe that many productive learning links and relations can be fostered through exploring lifewide assessment in physical education. We anticipate that many parents, coaches and others will recognise and want to engage with assessment tasks in physical education that are clearly designed to enhance a student's ongoing learning within and beyond school.

Reconceputalising assessment for learning in physical education: lifelong and lifewide

In this final section, we aim to bring together the insights and issues raised in our preceding discussion of lifelong and lifewide learning and, in so doing, extend thinking about assessment for learning in physical education. This chapter has been premised on our view that assessment as a pedagogical process can promote and support a conceptualisation of learning that is similarly process oriented and not bounded temporarily or spatially to schools or formal curriculum structures. We have highlighted that, in many respects, adopting a life*wide* approach to curriculum, pedagogy and assessment in physical education is an important and, arguably, critical step in developing a life*long* learning orientation. Ultimately, the development of assessment tasks and pedagogies in physical education needs to be concerned with both the breadth of learning contexts and opportunities that are part of students' current lives, and of those that they may encounter, desire to pursue and be enabled to access in the future. In further developing our discussion we therefore focus on a number of issues that we see as particularly important for this endeavour.

Personalised learning and assessment

In 2007 the Ministry of Education (MoE) in Aotearoa, New Zealand described personalised learning as 'central to the transformation that needs to occur in our education system in order to meet the needs of a 21st century knowledge society' (MoE, 2007, p. 18). Internationally, policy pronouncements have repeatedly highlighted the need for education systems, and curricula, that are designed for adaptability and responsiveness to individual needs, interests, abilities and personal circumstances (Penney, 2008). Following Hargreaves (2004), we emphasise that personalised learning needs to be understood and approached as a pedagogical process, in which assessment for learning has a key role to play.

Historically, senior secondary schooling has been the arena in which the concept of personalised learning has been most obviously taken up in physical education. It is a concept that has informed course developments in both Australia and the UK (see Kirk *et al.*, 2002, 2004), and been directly linked to curricula that have sought to promote Arnold's (1979) notion of learning 'about', 'through' and 'in' movement (e.g. QSA, 2010). This has informed curriculum design at the level of 'units of work' and individual lessons, with learning tasks focusing on personal experiences and seeking to extend students' personal skills, knowledge and understandings through participation in and analysis of those experiences. Reflecting the breadth of content encompassed in many senior secondary courses, such analysis has variously related to sociological, psychological, physiological or biomechanical issues or concepts, with course developers and teachers recognising that students are more likely to grasp disciplinary-based knowledge and understanding if they are able to relate it to personal experience. Curriculum design and pedagogy have thus sought to promote 'integration' of 'theoretical' and 'practical' dimensions of knowledge through personalised learning activities and, in this process, support students to draw on knowledge from various disciplines to extend their cognitive and embodied learning (see, for example, Thorburn, 2007; Thorburn and Collins, 2003).

This orientation in course developments can also be seen as having supported assessment being built into learning activities through staged/structured approaches and the development of assessment tasks that relate directly to personal 'real world' application and extension of learning. For example, as part of internal assessment for the Welsh Joint Examination Committee (WJEC) AS- and A-level[1] physical education courses, students produce a 'Personal Performance Profile' (PPP) incorporating self-assessment, targets for improvement, monitoring and evaluating progress towards targets and identifying next steps in developing personal performance. Students also undertake assessment as a coach, leader or official, in a 'rich task'. Thus, at AS-level, students selecting a competitive game activity are required to 'perform and either coach or officiate within a full-sided game, under competitive conditions, displaying all aspects of competency related to a specific position or role' (WJEC, 2008, p. 37).

The expectations detailed for each role point towards assessment that is directed towards the application of skills, knowledge and understanding in a role and context that should be personally meaningful, and with continued development in that role in mind (through the inclusion of critical analysis and evaluation). For example, students taking on the role of official are expected to:

- officiate within a full-sided game demonstrating the major rules and conventions;
- demonstrate a range of skills associated with officiating, such as, control, communicating, positioning;
- understand and implement any necessary safety requirements/procedures associated with the chosen activity (prior to/during/post);
- critically analyse and evaluate their own and others' performance, (players/other officials) e.g. in terms of decision making and consistency.

(WJEC, 2008, p. 37)

For this and the PPP task, the course specifications state that students will select one physical activity from those listed under the categories of 'sport', 'creative activities' and 'adventurous activities', further supporting the potential for assessment to support personally relevant learning. Yet, from our own experiences and research internationally, we are also aware that pragmatic considerations may mean that the options available to a group of students at a particular school may necessarily be more limited (Penney and Hay, 2008). Thus, while we see the WJEC course specifications and the above outline of task expectations as meaning that all students would potentially be able to link assessment with both a role and context that, from their individual life-wide and lifelong perspective, is the most authentic and personally meaningful, we are also hesitant in assuming that all students will be equally able to explore this potential. As we have discussed previously in exploring senior secondary course developments and assessment issues in different states within Australia, the activity contexts that students are able to focus on in seeking to develop their learning 'in', 'through' and 'about' physical education, and contexts that are able to be utilised for assessment purposes, are matters that have fundamental implications for equity and inclusivity in physical education. Activity contexts will influence the extent to which particular students' individual abilities are recognised, rewarded or, in contrast, effectively marginalised and, from a student perspective, deemed implicitly as lacking worth (Penney and Hay, 2008). If we return to our concern for assessment to align with not only personalised learning but also lifewide and lifelong learning, expectations such as those articulated in the WJEC text point to students being able to pursue a programme of learning that links learning in physical education lessons to learning in out-of-school contexts that *each student* identifies as most meaningful to their current and prospective future learning. To be effective, such a programme and its associated assessment activities will be negotiated and collaboratively developed with the student, teacher, coaches or leaders in the out-of-school context. The programme of learning and assessment should thus relate to the personal network of learning that each student can identify with, be shaped by the network and directed towards ongoing learning and participation in the network. From this perspective, the curriculum is developed across that network, pedagogical links are acknowledged as vital for student learning, and assessment will occur in contexts and ways that similarly support the personalised learning process. Assessment will then, necessarily, have inherent flexibility in relation to what the focus of assessment is at a given time, when, where and how a particular assessment task can best be progressed, and who is best placed to make judgements and provide feedback.

The irony we face is that, despite widespread recognition of the need for education generally and, arguably, senior secondary schooling particularly, to be personalised, connective and future oriented, thinking about curriculum, pedagogy and assessment remains invariably limited by traditional and formalised structures and systems. As Thorburn and Collins (2003) emphasised, successful implementation of conceptually sophisticated courses requires highly skilled, knowledgeable teachers. Furthermore, for advances in assessment 'for' lifelong and lifewide learning, we also need teachers willing and enabled to see beyond conventional arrangements and structures and to take 'pedagogical risks' in relation to assessment. Like Thorburn and Collins (2003), we emphasise that, unless there is systemic and structural support for such approaches, the progressive potential offered by either current or future curriculum is likely to remain underexplored. In many instances arrangements and requirements associated with summative and, particularly, externally examined assessment in senior secondary courses often appear to limit the extent to which either integration and personalisation or lifewide and lifelong learning perspectives can find expression in this particular arena and 'moment' of 'high-stakes' assessment. At the time when, educationally, assessment arguably needs to be very clearly focused on lifelong learning, neither the sorts of tasks nor the pedagogy of 'high-stakes' assessment will necessarily align with that vision. In Chapter 9 we further explore these issues in looking at recent curriculum developments and research in Western Australia.

Finally, we highlight that, while our discussion has focused on senior secondary physical education particularly, we certainly regard personalised, lifewide and lifelong perspectives as pertinent to curriculum, pedagogy and assessment for all phases of physical education. The opportunities to variously develop these agendas will undoubtedly be different in primary, junior secondary and senior secondary contexts, but the principles (such as the need for collaboration across contexts and with other pedagogues) that can guide the alignment of assessment for learning with students lives and learning in a holistic sense are likely to be common across phases.

Pedagogies of assessment for learning

Our preceding discussion has already identified that pedagogy has a key role to play in facilitating a learning orientation and, more particularly, lifewide and lifelong learning orientation in assessment. Here, we reiterate some of the pedagogical developments and approaches that we regard as most important in this regard. As reflected in our early discussion of assessment from lifelong and, secondly, lifewide perspectives, both self- and peer assessment can clearly support assessment focusing on learning and the individual learner. Engaging learners in assessment and enhancing their ownership of and responsibility for assessment are all important to achieving a sense of assessment being a process that is designed to support learning, and self- and peer assessment can both contribute towards this. As with any more learner-centred approaches in teaching, we stress the need for thorough planning and support for students to effectively take up new roles and responsibilities. Developments necessarily need to be progressive and will thus involve, for example, students progressing from a task involving them utilising an assessment checklist designed by the teacher, to discussion and development of criteria and checklists in groups and individual negotiation and development of assessment. As we proposed in Chapter 6, such engagement requires that students have the opportunity to develop their assessment literacy.

Negotiation and collaboration are further pedagogical characteristics of assessment that we see as fundamental to alignment with lifelong and lifewide learning. Initially, that negotiation and collaboration may be amongst students and between students and teachers. But, as indicated, for authenticity and in order to link learning in physical education with learning in students' wider lives, it needs to involve 'other pedagogues', associated with their participation in school, club and community sport and other physical activity, and associated with their family and friend networks. As we have emphasised throughout, conceptualising and positioning assessment as a shared endeavour to support learning across individual students' learning networks is a clear shift from perceptions of assessment as primarily concerned with making definitive judgements and/or something that is the sole domain and responsibility of teachers. Our anticipation and hope is that many parents, siblings, coaches and others will welcome greater openness about assessment in physical education and the chance to be actively involved in strategies designed to better support students' learning within and beyond schools. Once again, we do not pretend that innovation and change that relates to curriculum, pedagogy and assessment in physical education will be easy, quickly advanced or without many challenges. But we see this as a necessary step in advancing assessment for learning in physical education and as likely, in time, to bring considerable rewards for many students and everyone interested in supporting their learning. As with many developments in physical education, we anticipate that the greatest barrier to progress will be teacher time and we stress the need for systemic investment in and support for assessment pedagogies directed towards lifewide and lifelong learning.

Assessment for learning and 'real world challenges'

Our discussion throughout this chapter has been directed towards assessment having authenticity, relevance and meaning for students. We have discussed ways in which both the design and pedagogy of assessment tasks can be more clearly linked with students' current learning and lives beyond schools and, also, lifelong learning interests. In advocating that physical education focus on these links, we are aware that there is some danger in education being conceived of as servicing existing social and sporting structures with their inherent inequities left unchallenged and unchanged. Equity has always been to the fore of our work and remains so here. Thus, we stress that any development of assessment for lifewide and lifelong learning needs to simultaneously engage with and seek to reduce inequities in learning within and beyond physical education. We therefore advocate for a socio-critical orientation and a 'futures focus' that is underpinned by a commitment to greater equity in education, physical education and the societies in which they are set.

We recognise that there are some tensions in advocating developments in assessment that firmly connect with students' lives beyond schools and at the same time point to the need for assessment to be directed towards socio-critical and equity agendas. Yet, the two emphases are far from incompatible and, ultimately, we contend, must always be linked. For students to feel that they have influence over the direction that their learning and lives can take, learning needs to extend beyond 'servicing the status quo'. Students need to see that physical education can make a 'real' difference in and to their lives, in terms of what they feel they are able to do, experience and enjoy, now and in the future. For this to occur, assessment for learning must pursue lifewide and lifelong links with a socio-critical orientation. Assessment tasks need, therefore, to openly address inequities that students are variously aware of and experiencing amidst their learning and lives currently, and those that they may encounter in the future. The tensions and challenges that we are concerned with here are probably most clearly articulated in some of the work associated with Sport Education and hybrid models focusing on personal and social responsibility (Hastie and Buchanen, 2000), with learning experiences in Sport Education openly seeking a connection with and simultaneously promoting contrasts to the 'real world' of sport as it currently exists. We see assessment and, particularly, assessment that actively seeks collaboration and negotiation with 'other pedagogues' as, potentially, providing a prompt for changes in contexts beyond schools and, thus, a means via which we can pursue more and better learning opportunities for students. Assessment for learning from this perspective is, then, firmly oriented towards greater equity within and beyond physical education. It is recognised as a tool that can be utilised to generate discussions and new thinking about learning and learning opportunities in physical education within and beyond schools. It is concerned with quality and equitable learning opportunities and experiences now and in the future, for all students.

Concluding comments

This chapter has presented a case for lifewide and lifelong learning providing the basis for the reconceptualising of assessment for learning in physical education. It has once again pointed to the significance of alignment of curriculum, pedagogy and assessment in physical education, and the capacity for assessment to be something of a catalyst for changes in thinking and practices across curriculum, pedagogy and assessment. Attention has been drawn to pedagogies of assessment and the notion of personalised learning as potentially important avenues through which lifewide and lifelong orientations can be further developed in assessment in physical education. Throughout, the chapter has endeavoured to keep agendas of authenticity, efficacy and equity to the fore of rethinking what 'assessment for learning' in physical education might entail and be directed towards.

Having established and discussed these principles and their place in physical education assessment across the last two chapters, we now turn our attention to what they might look like in physical education practices. This is important to do as conceptual work is largely meaningless in the absence of concrete practice realities. Notably, in our next chapter we broaden our perspective on the place and practices of assessment beyond physical education to demonstrate the applicability of the principles and concepts we have proposed to the broader field of human movement studies (encompassing physical education), where the integration of psychomotor and cognitive learnings are markers of authentic practice and thus assessment.

9 Assessment innovations, transformations and technologies

Introduction

Effective and inclusive assessment practices need to be conceptually and theoretically robust and empirically informed. Where this is not so, the practices are vulnerable to problematic consequences including the employment of ill-informed pedagogies, propagation of unhelpful learnings about the subject and students' selves, and perpetuations of disingenuous perceptions regarding the merits of physical education. However, conceptually defensible assessment principles are of little use if they cannot be realised in practice. To demonstrate the applicability of the assessment principles that have been proposed in this book, we now turn our attention to examples of practice that represent an aspiration towards these principles in physical education and other fields of human movement such as sports coaching. By no means are these the only examples of 'good' or progressive assessment practice in physical education or human movement more generally. Rather, we have selected them because of their specific connection with the principles and issues that we have foregrounded in this book. Before we address the principles particularly, it is important to draw attention to some of the assessment innovations that have been developed and implemented in the field to date as they have made helpful contributions to the meaningful implementation of assessment in physical education.

The Teaching Games for Understanding (TGfU), and like teaching approaches such as the Tactical Games Model (TGM), have provided generative conceptual contexts for consideration of assessment. In particular the interest has been in providing teachers (and students) with tools that allow them to focus their attention on specific elements of performance within the inherently complex space of games implementation. Two notable tools for collecting information are the Game Performance Assessment Instrument (GPAI) developed by Oslin et al. (1998) and the Team Sport Assessment Procedure (TSAP) conceived of and validated by Grehaigne et al. (1997). These two initiatives represent assessment tools for gathering more-authentic information about students' capacities in movement contexts. More specifically, the GPAI was developed to assess 'game performance behaviours that demonstrate tactical understanding, as well as the player's ability to solve tactical problems by selecting and applying appropriate skills' (Oslin *et al.*, 1998, p. 231). Similarly, the TSAP was developed to assess game-play performance in team sports. Both these approaches made a significant advance on previous measures of performance in physical education such as skills drills and fitness tests that failed the test of ecological validity (as well as Messick's conditions for construct validity) and provided little information to teachers or students on specific points of focus for improvement or learning in games contexts. In this regard we agree with Memmert and Harvey (2008) who, while noting some points for further refinement of the GPAI, proposed that such work enhances 'our ability to make firmer conclusions about the effects of interventions that aim to improve both the individual and overall components of game performance' (p. 238).

Building upon these important contributions to assessment practice possibilities in physical education, we now aim to illustrate other contemporary assessment practices that perhaps more directly connect with the central principles we have proposed in this book, including the concerted and coherent alignment of assessment, curriculum and pedagogy and the satisfaction of the conditions of assessment efficacy. As we outlined in Chapter 7, these two principles are co-dependent and underpin assessment tasks and programmes that are learning oriented, authentic and integrated, valid and socially just. We will first look at the development of assessment in the context of models that we see as offering innovative potential for curriculum, pedagogy and assessment in physical education, including some of the implementation factors and considerations. Then we turn our attention to an assessment innovation that has been developed specifically with the conditions of assessment efficacy in mind, for application in psychomotor fields such as sports medicine and sports coaching, with potential for application in physical education assessment.

Assessment initiatives and physical education 'models'

When it comes to talk of 'models' in physical education, we are faced with terminology that has varied and been the subject of different viewpoints. Variously, Sport Education, for example, is referred to as a 'curriculum', 'pedagogical', 'curriculum and pedagogical' or 'instructional' model. In part the differences in terminology reflect cultural differences in the language of physical education. But the differences and, particularly, increasing problematisation of the terminology have also pointed to recognition that there is arguably a need to emphasise that Sport Education and other models simultaneously raise issues for curriculum and pedagogy, and their alignment. This text has been concerned with bringing assessment into this equation far more overtly and routinely in physical education. Thus, our stance is to regard Sport Education, TGfU, Teaching for Personal and Social Responsibility (TPSR) and other models that physical educationalists may adopt as, necessarily, models that span and provide a basis for better aligning curriculum, pedagogy and assessment. We also suggest that focusing on assessment efficacy, in the context of developing any particular model, offers important scope for further innovation in physical education practice.

Sport Education is a model that explicitly seeks contrasts to established practice in relation to the curriculum content (skills, knowledge and understandings) to be taught and learnt, curriculum structure (seasons) and aspects of pedagogy, emphasising, for example, greater student responsibility and leadership, use of structured group work and independent learning activities. There are clear links between the desire to engage students with new content and the ways that it is acknowledged that this can be facilitated. Thus, we see that learning associated with a range of roles (official, coach, journalist, etc.) requires learning experiences and approaches that position students in those roles and, in so doing, produce new pedagogical relations. Learning tasks associated with these various roles can, clearly, then be developed so as to link directly with assessment, in contexts and roles that can be seen by students as authentic. By providing students within teams with choices in relation to the roles that they wish to take up through a season, learning and assessment can also be personalised and serve to enhance the breadth of skills, knowledge and understandings that are signalled as of value in physical education. Yet, amidst and, in some respects, despite the different roles and the associated skills, knowledge and understandings that Sport Education can facilitate and promote, we remain aware that within contexts of competition, students' attention can very easily shift back to reflect dominant discourses and therefore focus on a far narrower range of learning than may be desired or intended in lessons. Sport education research and literature continues to reaffirm the clear opportunities but also considerable challenges associated with shifting the prime focus of learning to what may be seen as 'other' learning, such as social and/or personal skills, knowledge and understandings.

Assessment tasks and assessment pedagogies have, in our view, a key role to play in initiating and *sustaining* these sorts of shifts in learning and teaching focus in physical education. Specific tasks provide an explicit focus for learning from both teacher and student perspectives. They can therefore clearly signal value and status being accorded to skills, knowledge and understanding that, in a game context for example, students may not immediately associate with. Essentially, we have to recognise that, as soon as a particular game is selected as a learning context in physical education, the context and the specific performance-related motor skills associated with it will be to the fore of students' thinking. It will take conscious and explicit interruption to either extend or shift that thinking towards, for example, self-management or inter-personal skills. Assessment tasks embedded in and integral to learning activities can represent such interruption. Assessment pedagogy can in various ways then 'keep up' the interruption, to reinforce where students' attention needs to be directed. Teacher feedback to students during learning activities is a classic instance of pedagogy merging with assessment. Making 'on-the spot judgements' about students' learning and performance in a physical education lesson and communicating aspects of that judgement and, furthermore, the *implications* that the teacher sees that the judgement has for what students need to do to progress their learning are things that teachers should be doing consistently and, in many instances, as a matter of course in physical education. A teacher's reaction to something that they have seen, and the short comment to a student that follows, conveys and signals what learning they as a teacher are focusing on and want the student to focus on. 'On-the-spot' judgements can therefore be seen as 'assessment for learning'. To be effective as such, they need to be aligned with the learning focus established in and by curriculum and pedagogy. Thus, we suggest that feedback, which in essence is integral to teacher pedagogy, can actively support the desired learning focus of units of work or individual lessons. It can similarly reaffirm individual learning foci appropriate for any student. Alternatively, if a teacher's pedagogical focus slips back to more familiar learning foci and dominant discourses in physical education, feedback is then likely to detract from the agenda set for the unit, lesson or individual student.

Ongoing self- and peer assessment that is overtly targeted towards the skills, knowledge and understandings that are potentially perceived as 'other' may well prove another valuable strategy, and one that is often more powerful than teacher assessment in reaffirming the desired learning focus. Structured self-reflection journalling tasks, which may take written, oral, visual or a combined form, are again tools and techniques that have been utilised in Sport Education contexts, but by no means need to be confined to that model. Digital technologies and their expanded access have enhanced possibilities for students to routinely capture (on video, or via still camera shots, audio commentary or digital notes or drawings) 'evidence' relating to their performance and experiences in learning activities/tasks and then systematically review and reflect on that evidence. We suggest that structured review and reflection will be fundamental to students seeing such activities and the data gathered as 'assessment for learning'. Furthermore, as discussed in Chapter 8, technological developments also clearly extend the possibilities of bringing data from external contexts to inform learning 'within and beyond' physical education. The key issue we highlight in any such development is the need for the desired learning focus to be consistently reaffirmed by the tools used and all the pedagogues involved. As indicated, those may include peers, and peer judgements are again something commonly utilised in Sport Education. For example, students are often called upon to make judgements about officiating or fair play. But there are many opportunities and possibilities for peer 'assessment for learning' in Sport Education or physical education lessons based upon other models. The role and 'act' of peer assessment is arguably integral to team captain, coach and manager roles. Sport Education thus offers a framework via which students can actively and authentically explore two things: the implicit judgements that they are making in those roles about other students' abilities, performance and learning; and specific skills, knowledge and understanding that they can be prompted and supported to focus on (and that they may not otherwise have to the fore) in looking at peers. Both clear prompting and structured support (through mentoring and the provision of clear guidance and criteria for observation and judgements) are, in our view, critical aspects of a teacher's role and assessment pedagogy in order for peer assessment to be effective. In looking at the development of assessment for learning and assessment efficacy in Sport Education or physical education more broadly, we therefore reiterate Kim *et al.*'s (2006) emphasis that adopting new pedagogy will not be 'business as usual' for physical education teachers. Rather, it will involve considerable planning, require progressive development and professional learning support, and take time to reach the point of being part of the pedagogical repertoire that teachers, students and, prospectively, other pedagogues outside schools are all familiar and comfortable with.

Turning attention to a more specific example of efforts to shift the focus of teaching and learning in and through Sport Education, Ang *et al.*'s (2012) recent work focusing on the development of social and emotional learning provides a pertinent illustration of the detailed planning and sophisticated pedagogical skills that are needed to accord something such as social and emotional learning primacy in physical education. Their research drew attention to the challenges arising when, effectively, teachers are seeking to address multiple learning agendas simultaneously. In this instance, it was specific aspects of social emotional learning (SEL), alongside and amidst a recognised need to address learning relating to both the specific activity context being utilised and, also, the Sport Education framework and roles. We are not implying that assessment is some sort of 'silver bullet' for addressing these sorts of complexities. Rather, we see it as an essential and invaluable part of a curriculum and pedagogical process that is seeking to advance 'other' and inherently complex learning in physical education. Ang *et al.* (2012) drew upon Hellison's (1995) levels of responsibility to inform progression in the nature and demands of learning activities through a Sport Education unit and, in parallel, made explicit links to grade levels for learning articulated in the official text for Health and Wellbeing (as the learning area is termed) in the Australian state of Tasmania. In this respect, they clearly selected, appropriated and refocused particular discourses in their reading and utilisation of the official text. Further, in drawing on Hellison's work, they illustrated the way in which texts produced within the pedagogic recontextualising field can be brought into a productive relation with texts arising in the official recontextualising field, in order to generate 'alternative readings' of official texts (see Chapter 2). Such readings are, we contend, vital for the development of assessment practices in physical education that will be acknowledged as not only innovative but, critically, also legitimate.

Although here we have drawn upon work associated with Sport Education particularly, as indicated previously, we do not intend to imply that it is the only model offering possibilities for the development of assessment efficacy in physical education. To the contrary, we stress that the conditions for assessment efficacy can and should be actively explored in and through a variety of curriculum and pedagogical lenses that different models will provide.

An assessment initiative in Western Australia

We now turn to research that arose in the context of major curriculum reform in senior secondary schooling[1] in Western Australia (WA) and, more specifically, the development of new course specifications for Physical Education Studies (PES) in WA. The systemic reform acknowledged inequities in the long-standing senior secondary curriculum in WA and sought to enhance the learning and career opportunities available to all students through the development of some 50 new courses (Curriculum Council of Western Australia, 2002; Penney and Mr Walker, 2007). All of the courses were designed with the aim of providing for multiple learning pathways beyond senior secondary schooling, deconstructing a historical academic–vocational divide in senior secondary schooling in WA and, thus, catering for a diverse range of learners. Key features of the course design framework common to all new courses were flexibility in relation to the level at which students could follow a course and the opportunity to embed vocational qualifications into units of study and to select learning contexts to suit particular local community, school and student interests. Progressive agendas were, however, also contested amidst the development of the official texts (by agents in the official and pedagogical recontextualising fields) and could be seen as likely to be compromised by a policy decision that external examinations would be a compulsory aspect of assessment for all courses in order for them to count towards university entrance and by pragmatic and economic discourses associated with this decision (see Penney and Mr Walker, 2007; Penney *et al.*, 2011 for further discussion).

The research project initiated by the Centre for Schooling and Learning Technologies at Edith Cowan University (ECU) in collaboration with the Curriculum Council of Western Australia[2] reflected that physical educationalists were by no means alone in seeing the requirement for external examinations as potentially meaning that 'high-stakes assessment' would be in tension with curriculum goals and desired pedagogy. The new PES course design had actively sought to respond to the challenge of promoting integration of 'theoretical' and 'practical' knowledge in the curriculum, pedagogy and internal school-based component of assessment. Units of study (usually two per year) were incorporated and were intended to promote progressively more sophisticated linkages between multiple areas of content and enable students to explore and extend that content in and through various physical activity contexts. The school-based internal components of assessment encompassed three types of assessment and left open the matter of the physical activity contexts in which learning could be developed and demonstrated.

> **Performance/Response**: The assessment of students engaged in an activity, on-the-spot evaluation of performance and student reflective response

about their performance. Performance and reflection on performance in physical activity forms and settings, in the role of performer, coach and/ or official;

Investigation: Investigation of own and others' current participation in physical activity, participation potential, physical activity issues and social contexts. The findings may be communicated in any appropriate form e.g. written, oral, graphical, video, or various combinations of these; and

Response: Students apply their knowledge and skills when analysing and responding to a series of stimuli or prompts. Response to, analysis and evaluation of own or others' (peer or professional) participation in physical activity. Student responses may be oral, written or multimedia.

(Curriculum Council of Western Australia, 2008, p. 9)

It was intended that, at least to some extent, discourses of personalised learning and lifewide learning (see Chapter 8) would find expression in pedagogical practice and, more specifically, aspects of assessment. Embedding that potential in the official texts was neither assured nor simple to achieve and, ultimately, could be seen to go *some way towards* embracing these discourses, while falling short of openly privileging them. The matters of, for example, the contexts in which learning could legitimately (from a course perspective) be advanced and evidenced and, in turn therefore, whether programmes of learning could incorporate and, prospectively, be enhanced by external contexts of learning and 'other pedagogues' were contested within both official and pedagogical recontextualising fields. But external assessment and, specifically, the form and format that external examinations could and, indeed, should take in PES was the arena in which tensions between competing discourses was destined to be accentuated.

The 'Digital Forms of Assessment' research project recognised and sought to respond to this, in relation to the PES course and three other senior secondary courses within which 'performance learning' was deemed essential and core to the subject: Applied Information Studies; Engineering Studies; and Italian. In each instance, the project intention was to explore and demonstrate the pedagogical potential and pragmatic possibilities that the use of digital technologies in assessment could offer, such that requirements for validity and reliability in external assessment would also be met. While it is not possible to provide a detailed account of all aspects of the three-year project here, we can draw attention to some key features and findings. Drawing on other research internationally and insights from other subject areas, development of an external examination 'task' for the PES course took a staged/phased task approach and was designed to generate a portfolio of digital evidence in various formats, for any individual student.

Part 1. Structured online response to a tactical problem in a specific activity context: *text and graphic format responses.*

Part 2. Performance of four skills pertinent to the tactical problem: *video recordings of student performance.*

Part 3. Application of skills in a game/competitive performance context: *video recordings of student performance.*

Part 4. Structured online reflection on performance: *text and graphic format responses.*

The scope of learning addressed in and through the task was deliberately confined to a focus on particular aspects of course content (reflecting, primarily, the interests of the research partner organisation), but the potential for extension beyond this was openly acknowledged.

The task embraced the flexibility of the course in relation to prospective activity contexts in which it could be developed and implanted. Over the three years of the project the task was therefore adapted to and implemented in contexts including soccer, cricket, volleyball, swimming, rugby, netball and tennis (see Penney *et al.*, 2011 for further detail of the task development and adaptations).

The research demonstrated the potential for students to undertake a task that involved them directly applying aspects of 'theoretical' knowledge in practical performance and utilising personal performance as a focus and prompt to further explore and demonstrate that knowledge. Through the four parts, the task sought to establish and maintain a 'theory-prac' dynamic and generate evidence of learning that reflected and expressed that dynamic. For each student, the output of the task was four sets of digital data that were brought together into an individual portfolio of evidence for marking purposes. The assessment process attempted to retain a holistic, integrated learning orientation in that assessors were required to look across the portfolio of evidence in making judgements in relation to assessment criteria. In this respect, the research served to highlight the significance of both assessment criteria and assessment methods in terms of the messages generated about the forms of knowledge that will be recognised and valued in physical education. Penney *et al.* (2011) discussed the 'different judgement' that they saw arising from a 'comparative pairs' method of assessment compared to an 'analytical standards-based' method. In effectively requiring assessors to bring a collective body of evidence to bear in making a single judgement, 'integration' of knowledges was arguably foregrounded. The assessment criteria, method and judgement were directed towards this.

The research project makes no claims to have provided all the answers to long-standing dilemmas and tensions associated with summative and, particularly, external assessment in physical education. It has, however, provided an important illustration of the potential for research to directly link with and seek to inform the further development of innovation in curriculum development. From the outset, it also sought to clearly demonstrate the potential for external assessment to align with and support, rather than contradict, key aspects of curriculum design and intended pedagogy. The task that was developed sought to mirror the sorts of learning experiences that it was hoped students would increasingly be encountering in their PES lessons. In this respect the project openly acknowledged and sought to utilise the potential for external assessment to 'drive' thinking and practice relating to curriculum and pedagogy. It aimed to promote greater alignment of the three message systems through innovation in assessment. From an equity perspective, the task and assessment pedagogies it incorporated openly sought to extend the ways in which students could demonstrate their learning and abilities in physical education. Both students and teachers recognised and welcomed this (see Penney *et al.*, 2011).

This discussion of research and developments in assessment in senior secondary physical education in WA and those that follow below serve to highlight the potential that technologies offer to stimulate new thinking about possibilities for assessment in physical education and human movement more broadly. The use of video for assessment and pedagogy in physical education is becoming increasingly viable as school and student access to relevant devices becomes more widespread. Physical educators and researchers have the opportunity to invest in these technologies to support learning within the field rather than viewing them as a potential threat to the goals or work of the subject. This involves recognition of the fact that movement culture itself is increasingly imbued with technology use and reliance, which needs to be encompassed in physical education practices and has much to offer the optimisation of valid assessment in the subject.

Assessment efficacy in fields of human movement

Having considered models for the coherent and generative alignment of assessment, curriculum and pedagogy, and the technical and social factors affecting the design and implementation of such models, we now turn our attention to an assessment initiative that has been specifically informed by the conditions of assessment efficacy that were proposed by Hay and Penney (2009). This initiative is presented here for two reasons. First, the assessment protocol represents an example of practice that is conceptually and theoretically informed and that has been empirically evaluated. Second, it is an assessment innovation that has application in psychomotor fields other than physical education. This highlights the potential contributions that thinking and practice in physical education has to offer assessment practices in other fields such as medicine and sports coaching, but also reminds us of the situation of physical education within a broader human movement context. In this regard there is much that can be learnt from and applied to physical education and human movement more generally in relation to assessment principles and practices.

Hay *et al.* (2012) presented the evaluation findings of an innovative assessment protocol for the remote assessment of practical skills in sports medicine. The online clinical assessment of practical skills (*eCAPS*) protocol employed an underlying strategy involving the progressive organisation of 'assessment *as* learning' experiences that generated both formative and summative information on the execution of practical skills. The notion of 'assessment *as* learning' was proposed by Earl (2003), who argued that students learn through participating in assessment tasks and that this potential is as generative (and perhaps more so) as the information that is collected about students once the assessment task or programme is complete. The idea that student engagement in assessment can promote or even elicit valued learning situates assessment itself as a pedagogical endeavour rather than just a source of information for the service of various bureaucratic purposes. Informed by the pedagogical potential of assessment, the *e*CAPS protocol is organised into three interdependent elements (Figure 9.1).

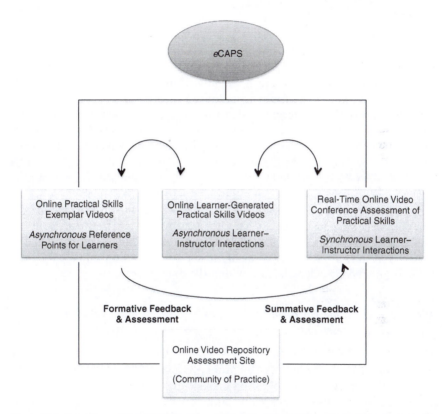

Figure 9.1 Overview of the *e*CAPS protocol (*Source*: Peter J. Hay, Craig Engstrom, Anita Green, *et al.* (2012). 'Promoting assessment efficacy through an integrated system for online assessment of practical skills', *Assessment and Evaluation in Higher Education*, 1–16, iFirst Article. Reproduced with permission).

Element 1: online practical skill-sets exemplars

This element of *e*CAPS involves the production and online provision of practical skill response exemplar videos by experts in the field. The suite of expert response exemplars are tailored to communicate and exemplify the authentic response characteristics expected of students in their online asynchronous and synchronous practical assessments (Elements 2 and 3 below). In this regard the exemplar online videos offer important information to students on how to perform the requisite skills as well as how to unpack and understand what the criteria, against which their practical performances are to be judged, look like in practice.

Element 2: learner-generated online video records of practical skills (asynchronous assessment)

With an intention towards promoting learner independence, the students are required to asynchronously produce and upload, to a private video-sharing website, a video clip of themselves performing the module-relevant practical skills. By asynchronous we mean that the skills are not performed by the students at the same time (or synchronously) as they are viewed by an assessor. This approach encourages students to undertake multiple replications of the practical skills-sets prior to uploading video materials for assessment, promoting student reflection and adjustment of their own skill execution. This element can be supported by the use of small and operationally simple hand-held digital camera devices (including those that come as standard features of most contemporary smart phones) that allow for easy, immediate review of recorded material and that facilitate rapid transfer of digital video information to a computer. The students' videos are then uploaded to a secure, password-protected online site that operates as a shared repository for students' demonstrations of their practical skills-sets. The assessors review and provide feedback (in video format) on student videos housed within the online repository.

Element 3: real-time video-conferencing assessment of practical skills (synchronous assessment)

In the third *e*CAPS element, students' practical skills are remotely assessed in real time (or synchronously) by an expert assessor through online video-conferencing (i.e. via Skype). During this person-to-person video conferencing the assessors are able to remotely prompt the students for more in-depth responses, ask for clarifications and then provide feedback to the students on their practical skills and associated knowledge immediately following the summative assessment experience.

To evaluate the efficacy of the *e*CAPS protocol, a short sports medicine module focusing on the physical examination of the knee joint was developed for implementation over a five-week period with a capped trial cohort of 40 second-year medical students. The students participated in the *e*CAPS trial on a voluntary basis, working within their normal ten-student Problem-Based Learning (PBL) groups, resulting in a 'blended' learning of online and face-to-face student interactions. The students received no instructional support during their engagement in the protocol and consequently their learning depended on their capacity to review their own and others' practical examination performances against the exemplars in order to produce a video of sufficient quality for assessment. A sample of randomly selected videos received expert feedback which needed to be interpreted and acted on by all students. Their performance quality was then summatively verified through the synchronous video conference (Element 3). Hay *et al.* (2012) demonstrated that the students' performances increased in the absence of direct instruction or contact with instructors. More significantly, the protocol itself promoted desired student interactions and behaviours, without the necessity for directions from an instructor.

In this regard the assessment sought to promote particular constructivist-based learning behaviours (Jonassen *et al.*, 1999) as well as provide a means of producing evidence upon which to make interpretations about student learning and performance quality. These intended behaviours included students' active involvement in the construction of knowledge; their interpersonal engagement in the process of knowledge construction; their increasing learning independence; and the ecological connectedness of their experiences (Hayes *et al.*, 2006). Hay *et al.* (2012) reported that the assessment protocol provided a flexible learning environment in which students engaged with the exemplar materials in varying ways, depending on their own general approaches to learning. The structure of the assessment process and the relationship between the exemplar videos (curriculum), the blended delivery format (pedagogy) and required video demonstrations of the students' practical skills (assessment) were important to the realisation of these desired learning behaviours. The fact that the students interacted and behaved as intended without direct prompt from the project leaders demonstrates the potential of tasks that are based upon the principles and aspirations of assessment efficacy to the learning of practical skills.

While the implementation and evaluation outcomes of *e*CAPS in the context of a second-year medicine knee joint examination module are in and of themselves noteworthy, the specific technologies used, as well as the basis and context of their utilisation and evaluation within the psychomotor domain, are of particular relevance for the field of physical education and other professional disciplines associated with human movement studies. *e*CAPS was constituted by the three elements involving (1) practical skills exemplar videos; (2) asynchronous assessment of videoed practical skills; and (3) real-time video assessment of those skills. That is, *e*CAPS was not fundamentally constituted by the musculoskeletal content of the project module and could be readily appropriated for the learning and assessment of other psychomotor-focused fields. In this regard, *e*CAPS could be utilised as a purely online protocol for the remote learning and assessment of practical skills or in a blended learning arrangement such as was trialled with the pre-clinical medical students.

It is in relation to blended learning and assessment that *e*CAPS has perhaps a major contribution to offer the field of physical education. In a school context, for example, groups of students could be given access to a suite of exemplar videos relating to movement skills and strategies in a particular sport or physical activity context. Requiring individuals and/or groups of students to review the exemplar online video materials and then produce and upload digital videos of their own specified performances would not only increase the learner-to-learner dialogue and independence, but would provide more tangible and valid evidence of student psychomotor learning in physical education. This latter outcome is particularly valuable for the subject as the enactment of valid and efficacious assessment in physical education has been problematic in the past (Hay and Macdonald, 2008). As we noted in Chapter 5, several studies have reported physical education assessment practices characterised by judgements made in the absence of valid and tangible evidence of student competence (Hay and Macdonald, 2008; Redelieus and Hay, 2009; Siedentop *et al.*, 2004). The absence of such evidence has limited not only the possible quality of the teacher judgements that are made, but also constrained the potential formative outcomes of assessment, including students' self- and peer assessments. The use of an online video repository of practical performance evidence allows students and teachers to populate and access *e*portfolios of achievement, increasing the volume and quality of performance evidence as well as providing obvious opportunities for external moderation of cohort standards (as is required in some high-stakes senior secondary school contexts, such as Queensland) (Hay and Macdonald, 2008). Of course, in a physical education class the synchronous component (Element 3) of *e*CAPS may constitute a variable aspect of the overall process. While Skype conferencing is unlikely to be necessary or readily utilised in physical education settings, the synchronous judgements of students by teachers (and readily captured synchronously on video) is a necessary condition of ecologically sound assessment practices. Moreover, the infrastructure and intent of this element could allow for cross-class/school interactions as well as moderation reviews of 'sample' student performances by external authorities.

The possibilities of *e*CAPS extend to other fields of human movement in which reproducible and accessible evidence of learning in the psychomotor and cognitive domains assist in learning and in the verification of practical competencies. Hay *et al.* (in press), for example, noted that the field of sports coaching had largely ignored the value of assessment to coach learning, development and accreditation, even though assessment is quite evident in official accreditation processes and in the work of coaches themselves as they select teams and offer feedback to athletes on their performances. The absence of reference to assessment is also notable given the burgeoning research and conceptual work that has been done in the area of coach learning and pedagogy. The value of utilising a model like *e*CAPS for coaching development and accreditation is that the learning and assessment responsibility is shifted to the developing coach in the context in which the development should be occurring. This is important as the context for the majority of coach learning is typically in the workplace, that is, doing coaching work (Gilbert and

Trudel, 2001; Lyle, 2002; Rynne *et al.*, 2009). Recent research into sports coach learning has unequivocally identified that coaching work is inherently multifaceted (Lyle, 2002). How coaches learn to coach to meet the highly fluid and dynamic nature of their work has its origins in a multivariate of experiences that could be more accurately captured than through the often employed approach of written accreditation 'tests'. The *e*CAPS approach is also valuable in the sense that the evidence collected is contextualised and reproducible, offering the opportunity for feedback as well as optimising the confidence of sporting organisations regarding the competence and applied knowledge of coaches at different levels.

Concluding comments

As we argued at the beginning of this chapter, assessment concepts and principles are of little merit if they are not practically plausible. In this chapter we have endeavoured to draw attention to assessment models and innovations that specifically exemplify the coherent planning of curriculum, pedagogy and assessment and the four conditions of assessment efficacy. The underlying aspiration of these approaches is the enactment of assessment that prioritises learning as an outcome of assessment engagement. Assessment with this focus can also and should also be able to generate quality information for making valid interpretations that serve other purposes such as the verification of competence, reporting of standards, selection, certification, etc.

Assessment has been increasingly prominent within the field of physical education. Sadly this has not been so in other human movement fields even though assessment is a notable feature of training in these fields (e.g. the assessment that undergraduate exercise scientists are engaged in as a part of their semester coursework) and in many cases the professional practices associated with them. We propose that the increasingly generative assessment work that is being conducted in physical education has much to offer the broader field of human movement studies in terms of theoretical and conceptual contributions as well as the application of assessment tools such as the GPAI and TSAP in other movement contexts such as sports coaching. However, we also believe that there is much that the physical education community can learn about assessment from work that has been conducted in other fields such as medical education, where an emphasis has been placed on enhancing the quality of assessment in the psychomotor domain. Clearly this requires both a broad engagement with assessment literature in and beyond school education as well as an open mind regarding the ways of applying this knowledge to the physical education context.

10 Conclusion

The purpose of this book has been to offer a theoretical perspective and conceptual orientation to an element of physical education practice that has been increasingly recognised within the international physical education community as important. As we have argued in preceding chapters, assessment in general has widely been acknowledged as a central element of institutional education, shaping curriculum and pedagogy in powerful ways and representing a critical reference point in political, professional and public debates about educational imperatives, outcomes and policy directions. The implications of assessment at a global and national level on the general curricular offerings of schools have also had an impact on the expectations of physical education from within and beyond its curriculum community. Internally, the matters of what subject knowledge, skills and understandings should be assessed, in what ways and at what points in a student's physical education remain widely contested. Furthermore, the factors informing these decisions within and beyond the subject have either been engaged with in a fragmented way or ignored altogether by many within the field. While there has been a notably steady increase in the research contributions to assessment in physical education in recent years (reflected in publications in academic journals in the field), we believe that a coherent conceptual framework for thinking about assessment practices, policies and research in physical education has yet to be adequately posed.

In responding to this need, we have considered the place and practices of assessment in physical education from a sociocultural perspective. We propose that this represents a fresh contribution to thinking in physical education that both galvanises the work that has already been conducted and offers new perspectives and principles that we believe will promote productive outcomes for physical education students and for the subject. We appropriated a sociocultural perspective first because we recognise that assessment is a social activity. As such we believe that a sociocultural perspective offers the most generative approach to understanding the practice of assessment in its broadest applications, while also allowing for more pragmatic attention to be given to assessment in the physical education class. A sociocultural approach to assessment draws attention to the purposes and outcomes of assessment at every level and in every context of an education system and reminds us that these purposes are constructed by people who have various interests at heart. In this regard it helps us to understand the relationship between these levels and contexts and the contribution that assessment makes to the communication between the levels and the content of those communiqués. Notably, a sociocultural perspective draws our attention to the impact of assessment on the macro and micro societies or social fields in which it is operational in relation to multiple purposes. We are provoked to consider the effects of assessment on people and quickly realise that assessment is not benign in its effects on the stakeholders engaged in its enactment or touched by its consequences, nor is it objective or straightforward. Assessment is complex in its development and impact, a fact that is often obfuscated by claims of the objectivity of particular measures or tools, or claims regarding their statistically defensible validity and reliability. Central to the challenge that a sociocultural perspective presents to these positivist perceptions of assessment is the fact that assessment itself is imbued with the values, beliefs and expectations of those designing the tasks, and that assessment impacts upon the views, values and understandings of those who are being assessed.

Necessarily, then, a sociocultural perspective on assessment shifts our primary focus away from the tools and techniques of assessment to view it as a whole *message system* that is influenced by and influencing the other two education message systems of curriculum and pedagogy. Viewing assessment as a message system brings to the fore the content and modes of communication of the social messages of education, through assessment. While we recognise that the technical aspects of assessment enactment are important to be well acquainted with, we have argued that doing so without first understanding the social and cultural situation and consequences of assessment is short sighted and sure to lead to some ambivalence towards the potential problematic outcomes of assessment on students, teachers and the subject, as well as underestimation of the contribution that assessment can make to the learning welfare of students in physical education.

Within this perspective we have taken cues from the work of Basil Bernstein, including his theory of the pedagogic device, to unpack and describe the way in which assessment works to designate and communicate value in the education system. As we demonstrated, this occurs at the macro level in terms of the value of subjects and various aspects of subject curricula, as well as at the micro level. Considering assessment as a message system, from a critical perspective, highlighted the effects of assessment as a communicator of value on the official constitution of the physical education curriculum, its enactment in schools and the possible pedagogical consequences of assessment on students' valuing of and engagement in the subject. These values can be explicit or implicit in their transmission. At the macro level, assessment serves as a marker of governmental and institutional value, where officially prescribed foci of assessment are positioned as elements of learning and practice warranting accountability. Elements of learning and practice for which accountability is not required are consequently positioned as of comparatively less significance. Such positioning has an influence on the operationalisation of the curriculum at the level of schools, where elements of the curriculum are afforded differential attention depending on the accountability imperatives associated with those elements. This includes the way in which assessment legitimises and promotes the acquisition, use and demonstration of certain knowledges over others and encourages particular forms of 'pedagogical work' (Tinning, 2009) in physical education.

Continuing with this framework, our attention was drawn to the nature and ways in which assessment policies and practices at various levels of the education system frame understandings and experiences in physical education, from teacher and student perspectives. The significance of assessment on the way in which students understand themselves and make sense of the valuing work of assessment is notable, particularly in relation to the way in which abilities are constructed and influence students' perceptions of likely or legitimate futures. Assessment plays a significant role in defining the social field values and consequential capitals of those fields through the officially sanctioned expectations of assessment practice and the official bases for interpreting the collected evidence, but most significantly through the engagement of teachers in the process of assessment. This means that, in order for assessment to be positively influential in physical education, teachers need to be knowledgeable and skilled in assessment and committed to enhancing students' own knowledge and skills in this area.

Key concepts and principles

In this book we have sought to establish some key assessment concepts and principles for understanding and promoting productive assessment practices in physical education. We built towards these principles by drawing on theoretical propositions that established the value of the coherent alignment of planning and implementing assessment, curriculum and pedagogy. From this point, taking lessons from the impact of assessment on the social fields of physical education classes and its consequences for cultural capital and ability construction, as well as our theorising of validity in physical education assessment, we arrived at a set of elements necessary for the *assessment literacy* of teachers and students in physical education. These four elements – assessment comprehension; assessment application; assessment interpretation; and critical engagement with assessment – provide a generative framework for centralising assessment in the work and practices of physical education teachers, promoting quality assessment practices, limiting the unintended consequences of assessment and empowering students in a practice in which power is inherently disproportionate.

Central to the knowledge that teachers and students should have in physical education were the conditions of *assessment efficacy*. Assessment efficacy draws directly on the assertions that assessment can work with curriculum and pedagogy to achieve desired educational ends. It is when the systems of curriculum, pedagogy and assessment are in tension with each other or disconnected that the problematic outcomes of assessment appear to be most pronounced. In particular, we drew insight from socio-critical perspectives on assessment highlighting its inevitable effects on students to propose that assessment can be structured in such a way as to intervene in the negative learnings that assessment can perpetrate but, more importantly, to provoke certain behaviours that have been shown to facilitate learning. We believe that there is more research work that can be done in this area.

Our notion of assessment efficacy has been deliberately tied to calls for the promotion of learning in physical education. Clearly this requires consideration of the nature and possible contexts of that learning. In this regard we contended that quality assessment tasks should provide students with opportunities to demonstrate the valued learnings defined by the curriculum 'in' and 'about' movement, without compromising the beneficial affective effects that may be realised 'through' movement. Furthermore, assessment should be supported by and an informant to, pedagogies that provide students with the requisite skills and knowledges to complete the tasks. We developed this understanding further through emphasising the contribution of assessment to 'lifelong' and 'lifewide' learning in physical education. We look forward to further reflection from the physical education community regarding the notions of assessment literacy and assessment efficacy in an endeavour to better understand assessment and its impact on the subject, students and society.

Training and professional development in assessment

Poor assessment practices are potentially damaging for students and physical education as a subject area. Ignorance and misunderstandings about assessment are arguably the most poignant reasons why such practices would persist in physical education. Reflecting the central role of assessment to the practices of contemporary education systems and our arguments that assessment should be repositioned in physical education so as to reflect a shared significance with curriculum and pedagogy, it would be necessary for pre-service and practising physical educators to better understand assessment from a theoretical, conceptual and practical basis. Again, we propose that assessment literacy and assessment efficacy, framed within an understanding of the necessary alignment and coherence of curriculum, pedagogy and assessment, provide useful reference points for planning pre-service teacher learning experiences and professional development opportunities for physical educators.

Reflecting the integrated elements of assessment literacy – knowledge, application, interpretation and critical engagement – for both PETE students and physical education practitioners, we propose that the following content may assist in supporting and, where necessary, enhancing assessment practices in physical education. This is not a comprehensive outline of possible content for a PETE course or professional development series, but provides some broad suggestions regarding content that may be helpful in optimising the impact of assessment. These knowledges and capacities may include:

- The operation of assessment as a message system in relation to curriculum and pedagogy: in education systems, generally; in physical education, specifically; in relation to the multiple purposes of assessment.
- Learning-oriented assessment practices, including the place and contribution of assessment to theories of learning; the connection of assessment to notions of lifelong and lifewide learning in physical education; mechanisms for generating and providing quality feedback to students.
- Theories and principles of validity in physical education assessment, including understanding the conditions of construct validity; collecting and managing assessment evidence.
- The impact of assessment on the social fields of physical education classes; optimising equity and social justice in physical education through assessment practices.
- Expected demonstrations of assessment task development and implementation in both the psychomotor and cognitive domains; use of established assessment tools such as the GPAI; efficacious appropriation of technologies for learning-oriented and authentic assessment.
- Referencing collected evidence against criteria and standards; social moderation of assessment interpretations; promoting reflective assessment practices.
- Approaches to developing physical education students' assessment literacy.
- Drawing on critical understandings of assessment as a message system; engagement in activities that bring to the fore teachers' values, beliefs and expectations about physical education and physical education students; and consideration of the impact of assessment on the way students are valued and positioned in the subject.

Focusing for a moment more specifically on professional development, consistent with the recommendations of Tsangaridou and O'Sullivan (1997), the assessment-focused training should connect with teachers' lived professional experiences. By this we mean that they should provide opportunities for teachers to share their understandings and approaches in a collegial and supportive forum that allows for the development of a working and shared understanding of assessment principles and practices. This could involve, for example, peer review of assessment tasks, criteria sheets and evidence collection processes, and moderation of grading decisions using reproducible forms of evidence. Moderation, in particular, whether an officially sanctioned process or a locally convened process, has been shown to be a powerful medium for enhancing the quality of teacher assessment practices as well as the reliability of their judgements (Cumming and Maxwell, 2004). Moderation involves the presentation of evidence for assessment decisions that have been made as a focal point for coming to consensus on the standards of the evidence provided. While it is most often associated with the process of grading, we believe that social moderation has much to offer teachers in the development of tasks and in the use of assessment in relation to curriculum and pedagogy endeavours.

The quality of physical education is dependent upon the quality of physical education teachers as marked by their practices. Given the relationship between curriculum, pedagogy and assessment, teachers' assessment capacities are thus central to the realisation of quality physical education. We encourage PETE instructors to review the content of assessment learning experiences of PETE students to ensure that their capacities are sufficient to minimise the unhelpful consequences of assessment and to situate its practise in such a way as to enhance the experiences and outcomes of every physical education student. In relation to ongoing professional learning, we recognise that there are significant costs associated with the development and delivery of courses. However, we would encourage professional teaching associations to give greater consideration to assessment as a topic for professional learning as a means of also optimising other facets of physical education practice. Certainly, providing a context or medium for physical education teachers to discuss and share assessment practices is an important step to supporting assessment efficacy as a goal for physical education teachers.

Further considerations and discussions

This book has been presented as a step towards such understanding but, also, towards the optimisation of the potential that assessment presents to contribute to the realisation of the aims of a physical education. The potential for assessment to be recognised and employed as a catalyst for pedagogical change towards greater equity in physical education is something that we view as important to consider further in arenas of policy, practice and research. With this in mind, there is much scope for further research and conceptual work to be conducted in the area of physical education assessment. While we have advocated a sociocultural perspective in this book, we recognise that other perspectives and the methodologies they are typically connected with can also make valuable contributions to research in this area. In this section we take the opportunity to propose some possible directions for further discussion, conceptualisation and empirical work that connects with and extends the concepts and principles proposed in this book. In this regard it offers a suggested guide towards advancing physical education assessment thinking and impact.

There are numerous factors that contribute to the assessment message system. These factors may include, for example, national socio-political dis-courses, the investments of key stakeholders in the constitution and proposed outcomes of the curriculum and the structure of systemic accountability mechanisms. Arguably the most powerful but perhaps the least understood in the field of physical education is the globalisation of education itself. Much of the international comparative work that has been done in physical education has focused on the practices and place of physical education in different countries without paying sufficient attention to what Lingard *et al.* (2005) have described as the discourses and dynamics of the emerging 'global education policy field'. In focusing attention this way, Lingard *et al.* (2005, p. 760) claimed:

> In effect, the concept of educational policy as a field has multiple levels, one of which includes a global character under the increasing influence of international agencies such as the World Bank, Organisation for Economic Co-operation and Development (OECD) and UNESCO. We argue here that the structure, scope and function of educational policy have changed with the attention paid to the role of education in economic growth and innovation by these agencies. Here we use the word 'global' to designate a level of policy connection above the national. Policy debates at this level should be recognized to constitute a separate level within a global policy field in education.

Viewing education from a globalisation perspective will better inform physical education researchers' understandings of the way in which a global policy field has emerged and shaped what is operational as educational capital, internationally and within nation-states (Rizvi and Lingard, 2010). In relation to this understanding, we believe that advocacy for the mere presence of assessment in physical education (almost irrespective of the 'stakes') misses the large and powerful discourses shaping what is and will be understood as education, schools and schooling in the future. A futures-oriented perspective on physical education must look beyond the internal machinations and constitutions of physical education curricula to account for these factors and must acknowledge the significance and influence of assessment on the configurations and reconfigurations of education, globally and locally. This requires understanding of the socio-political discourses and international economic imperatives that are active as they inform policy and practice decisions at these levels.

Moving from an international perspective to a more systemic view, we propose that further research work focused on the ways in which assessment foci and practices are recontextualised at different levels of the pedagogic device is necessary to both understand the impact of assessment on what is valued in the curriculum at the system, school and classroom level and to better understand the processes at play through assessment that result in the production, recontextualisation and reproduction of pedagogic discourses. On the one hand this is proposing the need for further critical engagement with assessment across the system, including the relationship between the macro and micro contexts and their implications for teacher practice and student potential. However, on the other hand it also represents a particular interest in *assessment fidelity*. By this we refer to the relationship between the official, intended and enacted assessment processes and the factors that affect the way these processes change. Of course, as we demonstrated in Chapters 4 and 5, this has particular influence over the configuration of abilities and the valid practices of assessment in physical education. However, more conceptual work is needed to unpack what could be conceived of or tolerated as 'fidelity' and the factors that impact on its realisation in the subject.

As we proposed in Chapter 6, there is important research work to be done ascertaining the current levels of teacher and student assessment literacy and the sources of their understandings. Connected with such work are the obvious discussions about our proposed elements of assessment literacy to which we invite further comment and development. We recommend that action research has much to offer in the exploration of the impact of enhancing students' assessment literacy on their assessment experiences. Furthermore, such a research effort could provide further valuable information on the way assessment informs students' beliefs about their abilities and the abilities of others, as well as the way they value and engage in physical education and movement culture outside the physical education classroom as a consequence of their assessment experiences. Such work should be conducted in diverse demographic contexts to capture the specific needs of students in different social groupings and as an opportunity to better understand physical education and assessment in relation to constructs such as class, gender and ethnicity.

In arguing for a sociological rethink of the nature of ability in schools, Evans (2004) explained that 'schools build on and reproduce, rather than produce, "ability"; they identify and endorse those individual characteristics that parents invest in, differently, by virtue of their social class' (p. 99). That is, the class context of the school is important for the way abilities are realised and recognised. He further suggested that the significance of stratifying technologies of education for the reproduction of 'achievement, under-achievement, educational aspirations, "ability" and identity in contexts of physical education requires detailed exploration' (p. 99). Necessary, then, in understanding conceptions and constructions of abilities (and their potential educational consequences for practices such as criteria- and standards-referenced assessment) is an examination of the social class contexts of the schools and the specific educational modalities (Bernstein, 1996) of the schools. We were unable to find any reported engagement with assessment and physical education that focused specifically on social class. This presents an obvious avenue for further empirical attention.

Given the importance of a certain quality of evidence for assessment in the performance domain we believe that it is also timely for the physical education community to give more concerted attention to the use of information and communication technologies (ICTs) in physical education to support the efficacy of assessment, curriculum and pedagogy in the subject. Just as assessment has increasingly been centralised in the practices of education, the integration of ICTs in teaching and learning has become an entrenched expectation of contemporary educational work, reflecting their pervasive presence in the broader community. The ubiquity of ICTs in both civic and vocational realms and their centrality to the emergent knowledge economies and information societies of industrialised nations (Nesbit and Winne, 2008; Pelgrum and Plomp, 2004) has provoked considerable international education policy efforts towards increasing the integration of ICTs into mainstream education (Varvel *et al.*, 2007). In this regard, Nesbit and Winne argued that the emerging information society itself 'not only introduces more efficient means to acquire knowledge and skills, it also defines new knowledge and skills that demand recognition and accommodation within our education systems' (2008, p. 174).

In contrast to literature on contemporary digital technology within general education, rigorous conceptual, theoretical and empirical research work in physical education is comparatively sparse. The nature of scholastic engagement with such technology in physical education has also been somewhat narrow. In the first instance, almost all the literature pertaining to the use of ICTs in physical education has originated in the USA. In contrast, academic avenues for the dissemination of scholarly physical education work in Europe, Asia and Australia have been notably bereft of both research into the impact of ICTs in physical education as well as conceptual and polemic pieces regarding their contribution to curriculum or assessment in the field. Of the literature that is available, most of it is found in professional journals as opposed to research-specific journals and focuses heavily on the pedagogical potential of technology. Examples of proposed ICT pedagogical possibilities have included ideas for using personal digital assistants (PDAs) to assist in planning and assessment practices (e.g. DerVanik, 2005), the value of digital video recorders to assist in the provision of feedback to physical education students on their skill execution (e.g. Lim *et al.*, 2009), rationales and planning ideas for using computer-based heart rate monitors (e.g. Nichols *et al.*, 2009) and the potential of 'exergaming' for increasing student engagement and interest in physical education and physical activity more generally (e.g. Staiano and Calvert, 2011). As we proposed in Chapter 9, ICTs are now much more financially accessible to schools and students and allow for better collection, storage and access to assessment, curriculum and pedagogy-related information. However, our advocacy for the promotion of technology is made with a caveat that the appropriation of technologies is both directly tied to a coherent alignment of curriculum, assessment and pedagogy, and informed by robust theoretical, conceptual and empirical contributions.

Finally, we would like to encourage the physical education community to look beyond its 'boundaries' to draw from productive practices in mainstream education, but more specifically from health-oriented fields that also involve assessment of students' psychomotor capacities. Furthermore, as we demonstrated with the *e*CAPS model, thinking in the field of physical education (in this case, Hay and Penney's proposed conditions of assessment efficacy) has much to offer assessment practices in these fields. This is no more evident than in the broader field of human movement studies (or kinesiology, as it is referred to in other places such as the USA), where very little, if any, specific attention has been directed towards the assessment of human movement studies students, or the assessment capacities of practitioners exiting these degree courses. There is significant scope for research in this area as well as the application of efficacious assessment practices developed in physical education for these fields. Already this need is being recognised in international sports coaching thinking, with promising opportunities for research and engagement in this field. We encourage others in the field of physical education to also broaden their thinking about assessment and its contribution to other contexts of psychomotor learning.

An invitation

This book is by no means the definitive statement on assessment in physical education. Nevertheless, we believe that it offers an important perspective on assessment that both recognises the limitations of assessment and moves our thinking towards the ways in which the practice can benefit students in physical education, as well as the subject itself. In this regard we have viewed assessment as offering *transformative* influence in relation to the orientation, content and delivery of physical education. Fundamentally, our project has been to shed light on the vast influence of assessment beyond, towards and within physical education to provide a more generative reference point for practical and technical considerations of assessment. We encourage the physical education community to engage in further debate, discussion and empirical efforts related to assessment in order to optimise the practice itself, but more significantly to strengthen physical education as a professional endeavour and as a valued field of learning in systemic curriculum thinking.

Notes

2 Producing assessment messages

1 We note that Bernstein's 1990 text used American spelling for e.g. specialization, recontextualization, while his 2000 text used English spelling, e.g. specialisation, recontextualisation. We have retained the original format in direct quotations from texts and, beyond this, adopt English spelling.

3 Definitions, differentiations and communications of assessment

1 The OP is a tertiary entrance score, the bands of which range from '1' (the most valued score) to '25'. Although the school-based assessment is said to be criteria and standards referenced, the OP score bands follow a 'normal curve' distribution.

7 Aligning curriculum, pedagogy and assessment in physical education

1 General Certificate of Secondary Education.

8 Reconceptualising assessment for learning in physical education

1 AS refers to 'Advanced Subsidiary' and A refers to 'Advanced' level courses in senior secondary schooling in England and Wales. WJEC is one of several examination boards offering AS- and A-level-accredited courses. The choice of examination board and specific courses offered is a school decision.

9 Assessment innovations, transformations and technologies

1 Secondary school education in Western Australia encompasses grades 7 to 12. The students are aged between 12 and 18.
2 The 'Digital Forms of Assessment' research project was supported by a grant from the Australian Research Council and the Curriculum Council of Western Australia. The team was led by Paul Newhouse and John Williams and included senior researchers, Dawn Penney, Cher Ping Lim, Jeremy Pagram, Andrew Jones, Martin Cooper, Alistair Campbell, project manager Mel Brewer and many research assistants. The work of everyone in this team has contributed to the research outcomes reported.

References

Ang, S. C., Penney, D. and Swabey, K. (2012). Pursuing social and emotional learning outcomes through sport education: An Australian case study. In P. Hastie (Ed.), *Sport education: International perspectives* (pp. 116–32). London: Routledge.

Annerstedt, C. and Larsson, S. (2010). 'I have my own picture of what the demands are ... ': Grading in Swedish PEH – problems of validity, comparability and fairness, *European Physical Education Review*, 16(2), 97–115.

Apple, M. W. (2004). *Ideology and curriculum*. London: RoutledgeFalmer.

Arnold, P. J. (1979). *Meaning in movement, sport and physical education*. London: Heinemann.

—— (1988). *Education, movement and the curriculum*. London: The Falmer Press.

Azzarito, L. and Solomon, M. A. (2005). A reconceptualization of physical education: The intersection of gender/race/social class, *Sport, Education and Society*, 10(1), 25–47.

Bachman, L. F. (2002). Alternative interpretations of alternative assessments: Some validity issues in educational performance assessments, *Educational Measurement: Issues and Practice*, 21(3), 5–18.

Ball, S. J. (1990). *Politics and policy making in education: Explorations in policy sociology*. London: Routledge.

—— (1998). Big policies/small world: An introduction to international perspectives in education policy, *Comparative Education*, 34(2), 119–30.

—— (2003). The teacher's soul and the terrors of performativity, *Journal of Education Policy*, 18(2), 215–28.

Benjamin, S. (2003). What counts as 'success'? Hierarchical discourses in a girls' comprehensive school, *Discourse: Studies in the Cultural Politics of Education*, 24 (1), 105–18.

Bentley, T. (1998). *Learning beyond the classroom: Education for a changing world*. London: Routledge.

Berliner, D. C. (2006). Our impoverished view of educational research, *Teachers College Record*, 108(6), 949–95.

Bernstein, B. (1971). *Class codes and control*. London: Routledge.

—— (1990). *The structuring of pedagogic discourse, Vol IV: Class, codes and control*. London: Routledge.

—— (1996). *Pedagogy, symbolic control and identity. Theory, research and critique*. London: Taylor & Francis.

—— (2000). *Pedagogy, symbolic control and identity. Theory, research and critique*. Maryland: Rowman & Littlefield.

Black, P. and Wiliam, D. (1998). Assessment and classroom learning, *Assessment in Education*, 5(1), 7–73.

—— (2006). Developing a theory of formative assessment. In J. Gardner (Ed.), *Assessment and learning* (pp. 81–100). London: Sage.

—— (2009). Developing the theory of formative assessment, *Educational Assessment, Evaluation and Accountability*, 21(1), 5–31.

Blomqvist, M., Vanttinen, T. and Luhtanen, P. (2005). Assessment of secondary school students' decision-making and game-play ability in soccer, *Physical Education and Sport Pedagogy*, 10(2), 107–19.

Bonal, X. and Rambla, X. (2003). Captured by the totally pedagogised society: Teachers and teaching in the knowledge economy, *Globalisation, Societies and Education*, 1(2), 169–84.

Bourdieu, P. (1986). The forms of capital. In J. Richardson (Ed.), *Handbook of theory and research of the sociology of education* (pp. 241–58). Westport, CT: Greenwood.

—— (1989). Social space and symbolic power, *Sociological Theory*, 7(1), 14–25.

—— (1990). *Sociology in question*. Cambridge: Polity Press.

—— (1996). *The state nobility: Elite schools in the field of power*. Oxford: Polity.

Bowe, R. and Ball, S. J., with Gold, A. (1992). *Reforming education and changing schools: Case studies in policy sociology*. London: Routledge.

Broadfoot, P. M. (1996). *Education, assessment and society*. Buckingham: Open University Press.

——(1998). Quality standards and control in higher education: What price life-long learning?, *International Studies in Sociology of Education*, 8(2), 155–80.

Broadfoot, P. M. and Black, P. (2004). Redefining assessment? The first 10 years of *Assessment in Education*, *Assessment in Education*, 11(1), 7–27.

Brookes, C. (2004). Forward. In D. Hargreaves, *Learning for life: The foundations for lifelong learning*. Bristol: Policy Press.

Brown, G. T. L. (2004).Teachers' conceptions of assessment: Implications for policy and professional development, *Assessment in Education*, 11(3), 301–18.

Brown, T. D. and Penney, D. (2011). *Learning 'in', 'through' and 'about' movement in senior physical education? The new VCE PE*. Paper presented at the AIESEP Moving People, Moving Forward International Conference, 22–25 June, University of Limerick. (Retrieved from <www.iccbookings.com/AIESEP2011/AIESEP% 202011%20Conference%20Proceedings.pdf>).

Caldas, S. J. and Bankston, C. (1997). Effect of school population socioeconomic status on individual academic achievement, *Journal of Educational Research*, 90(5), 269–77.

Cole, D. A., Martin, J. M., Peeke, L. A., Seroczynski, A. D. and Fier, J. (1999). Children's over and underestimation of academic competence: A longitudinal study of gender differences, depression and anxiety, *Child Development*, 70(2), 459–73.

Connolly, P. (2006). The effects of social class and ethnicity on gender differences in GCSE attainment: A secondary analysis of the Youth Cohort Study of England and Wales 1997–2001, *British Educational Research Journal*, 32(1), 3–21.

Connolly, P. and Healy, J. (2004). Symbolic violence, locality and social class: The educational and career aspirations of 10–11-year-old boys in Belfast, *Pedagogy, Culture and Society*, 12(1), 15–33.

Cumming, J. J. and Maxwell, G. S. (1999). Contextualising authentic assessment, *Assessment in Education: Principles, Policies and Practices*, 6(2), 177–194.

—— (2004). Assessment in Australian schools: Current practice and trends, *Assessment in Education*, 11(1), 89–108.

Curriculum Council of Western Australia. (2002). *Our youth, our future: Post-compulsory education review*. Perth: Curriculum Council of Western Australia.

—— (2008). *Physical Education Studies 2008*. Perth: Curriculum Council of Western Australia.

Darling-Hammond, L. (2010). *The flat world and education: How America's commitment to equity will determine our future*. New York: Teachers' College Press.

Davies, B. (1995). Acquiring the means of acquisition: Is pedagogic practice a crucial variable? *International Studies in Sociology of Education*, 5(2), 189–202.

Department for Education (2011). Physical education (PE) attainment target level descriptions. (Retrieved on 18 February 2012 from <www.education.gov.uk/schools/teachingandlearning/curriculum/secondary/b00198952/pe/ks4/attainment>.)

DerVanik, R. (2005). The use of PDAs to assess in physical education, *Journal of Physical Education, Recreation and Dance*, 76(6), 50–52.

Dunne, M. and Gazeley, L. (2008). Teachers, social class and underachievement, *British Journal of Sociology of Education*, 29(5), 451–63.

Earl, L. M., (2003). *Assessment as learning: Using classroom assessment to maximise student learning*. Thousand Oaks, CA: Corwin Press.

Evans, J. (2004). Making a difference? Education and 'ability' in physical education, *European Physical Education Review*, 10(1), 95–108.

Evans, J. and Penney, D. (1995). The politics of pedagogy: Making a National Curriculum Physical Education, *Journal of Education Policy*, 10(1), 27–44.

—— (2008). Levels on the playing field: The social construction of physical 'ability' in the physical education curriculum, *Physical Education and Sport Pedagogy*, 13(1), 31–47.

Evans, J., Rich, E. and Holroyd, R. (2004). Disordered eating and disordered schooling: What schools do to middle class girls, *British Journal of Sociology of Education*, 25(2), 123–42.

Evans, J., Rich, E., Davies, B. and Allwood, R. (2005). The embodiment of learning: What the sociology of education doesn't say about risk in going to school, *International Studies in Sociology of Education*, 15(2), 129–48.

Fitzclarence, L. and Tinning, R. (1990). Challenging hegemonic physical education: Contextualising physical education as an examinable subject. In D. Kirk and R. Tinning (Eds), *Physical Education, curriculum and culture: Critical issues in the contemporary crises* (pp. 169–91). London: Falmer Press.

Flintoff, A. (2008). Targeting Mr Average: Participation, gender equity and school sport partnerships, *Sport, Education and Society*, 13(4), 393–411.

Freebody, P. and Luke, A. (1990). Literacies programs: Debates and demands in cultural context, *Prospect: Australian Journal of TESOL*, 5(7), 7–16.

—— (2003). Literacy as engaging with new forms of life: The 'four roles' model. In G. Bull and M. Anstey (Eds), *The literacy lexicon* (2nd edn) (pp. 51–66). Australia: Prentice Hall.

Fry, J. M. and McNeil, M. C. (2011). 'In the nation's good': Physical education and school sport in Singapore, *European Physical Education Review*, 17(3), 287–300.

Fullan, M. (2002). The role of leadership in the promotion of knowledge management in schools, *Teachers and Teaching: Theory and Practice*, 8(3), 409–19.

—— (2000). The three stories of educational reform: Inside; inside/out; outside/in, *Phi Delta Kappan*, 81, 581–84.

Gagne, F. (1999). My convictions about the nature of abilities, gifts and talents, *Journal for the Education of the Gifted*, 22(2), 109–36.

Gale, T. (2003). Realising policy: The who and how of policy production, *Discourse: Studies in the Cultural Politics of Education*, 24(1), 51–65.

Gerwitz, S. (1998). Conceptualizing social justice in education: Mapping the territory, *Journal of Education Policy*, 13(4), 469–84.

Gibson, P., Okely, A. D., Webb, P. and Royall, B. (1999). Talent identification in rugby union, *ACHPER Healthy Lifestyles Journal*, 46(4), 5–10.

Gilbert, W. D. and Trudel, P. (2001). Learning to coach through experience: Reflection in model youth sport coaches, *Journal of Teaching in Physical Education*, 21, 16–34.

Gipps, C. (1994). *Beyond testing: Towards a theory of educational assessment*. London: The Falmer Press.

—— (1999). Socio-cultural aspects of assessment, *Review of Research in Education*, 24, 355–92.

Glover, S. (2001). The social construction of pedagogic discourse in health and physical education: A study of writing the national statement and profile 1992–94. Ph.D. thesis, University of Queensland, QLD.

Goodson, I. (1997). *The changing curriculum: Studies in social construction*. New York: Peter Lang.

Green, K. (2001). Examinations in physical education, a sociological perspective on a new 'orthodoxy', *British Journal of Sociology of Education*, 22(1), 51–73.

—— (2005). Examinations: A 'new orthodoxy' in physical education? In K. Green and K. Hardman (Eds), *Physical education: Essential issues* (pp. 98–110). Thousand Oaks, CA: Sage.

Grehaigne, J.-F., Godbout, P. and Bouthier, D. (1997). Performance assessment in team sports, *Journal of Teaching in Physical Education*, 16(4), 500–16.

Hardman, K. (2008). Physical education in schools: A global perspective, *Kinesiology*, 40(1), 5–28.

Hardman, K. and Marshall, J. J. (2000). *World-wide survey of the state and status of school physical education*. Manchester: University of Manchester.

Hargreaves, D. (2004). *Learning for life*. Bristol: Policy Press.

Hart, S. (1998). A sorry tail: Ability, pedagogy and educational reform, *British Journal of Educational Studies*, 46(2), 153–68.

Hastie, P. (Ed.). (2012). *Sport education: International perspectives*. Abingdon, Oxon: Routledge.

Hastie, P. and Buchanen, A. M. (2000). Teaching responsibility through sport education: Prospects of a coalition, *Research Quarterly for Exercise and Sport*, 71(1), 25–35.

Hay, P. J. (2006). Assessment for learning in physical education. In D. Kirk, D. Macdonald and M. O'Sullivan (Eds), *The handbook of physical education* (pp. 312–25). London: Sage.

Hay, P. and lisahunter (2006). 'Please Mr Hay, what are my (poss)abilities?': Legitimation of ability through physical education practices', *Sport, Education and Society*, 11(3), 293–310.

Hay, P. J. and Macdonald, D. (2008). (Mis)appropriations of criteria and standards-referenced assessment in a performance-based subject, *Assessment in Education: Principles, Policy and Practice*, 15(2), 153–68.

Hay, P. J. and Penney, D. (2009). Proposing conditions for assessment efficacy in physical education, *European Physical Education Review*, 15(3), 389–405.

Hay, P. J. and Macdonald, D. (2010). Evidence for the social construction of ability in physical education, *Sport, Education and Society*, 15(1), 1–18.

Hay, P. J., Dickens, S., Crudgington, B. and Engstrom, C. (in press). Exploring the potential of assessment efficacy in sports coaching, *International Journal of Sports Science and Coaching*.

Hay, P. J., Engstrom, C., Green, A., Friis, P., Dickens, S. and Macdonald, D. (2012). Promoting assessment authenticity and efficacy through an integrated system for online clinical assessment of practical skills, *Assessment and Evaluation in Higher Education*, DOI:10.1080/02602938.2012.658019.

Hayes, D., Mills, M., Christie, P. and Lingard, B. (2006). *Teachers and schooling making a difference.* Sydney: Allen & Unwin.

Hellison, D. (1995). *Teaching responsibility through physical activity.* Champaign, IL: Human Kinetics.

Hensley, L. D., Lambert, L. T., Baumgartner, T. A. and Stillwell, J. L. (1987). Is evaluation worth the effort?, *Journal of Physical Education, Recreation and Dance*, 58(6), 59–62.

Herrington, J., Oliver, R. and Reeves, T. C. (2003). Patterns of engagement in authentic online learning environments, *Australian Journal of Educational Technology*, 19(1), 59–71.

Hodge, G. M., McCormick, J. and Elliot, R. (1997). Examination-induced distress in a public examination at the completion of secondary schooling, *British Journal of Educational Psychology*, 67(2), 185–97.

Hunter, I. (1994). *Rethinking the school: Subjectivity, bureaucracy, subjectivity.* St Leonards, N.S.W: Allen & Unwin.

Hunter, L. (2004). Bourdieu and the social space of the PE class: Reproduction of doxa through practice, *Sport, Education and Society*, 9(2), 175–92.

Hursh, D. (2008). *High-stakes testing and the decline of teaching and learning.* New York: Rowman & Littlefield.

Jeffrey, B. (2002). Performativity and primary teacher relations, *Journal of Education Policy*, 17(5), 531–46.

Jenkins, R. (2002). *Pierre Bourdieu.* London: Routledge.

Jonassen, David H., Peck, Kyle L. and Wilson, Brent G. (1999). *Learning with technology: A constructivist perspective.* New Jersey: Merrill.

Jones, S. and Myhill, D. (2004). 'Troublesome boys' and 'compliant girls': Gender identity and perceptions of achievement and underachievement, *British Journal of Sociology of Education*, 25(5), 547–61.

Kane, M. T. (2001). Current concerns in validity theory. *Journal of Educational Measurement*, 38(4), 319–42.

——(2006). Validation. In R. L. Brennan (Ed.), *Educational measurement* (4th edn) (pp. 17–64). Westport, CT: American Council on Education/Praeger Publications.

Kenway, J. and Bullen, E. (2001). *Consuming children: Education – entertainment – advertising.* Buckingham: Open University Press.

Kim, J., Penney, D., Cho, M. and Choi, H. (2006). 'Not business as usual': Sport education pedagogy in practice, *European Physical Education Review*, 12(3), 361–79.

Kinchin, G. D. (2001). Using team portfolios during a sport education volleyball season, *Journal of Physical Education, Recreation, and Dance*, 72(2), 41–44.

Kincheloe, J. L. and McLaren, P. L. (1994). Rethinking critical theory and qualitative research. In N. K. Denzin and Y. S. Lincoln (Eds), *Handbook of qualitative research* (pp. 138–57). Thousand Oaks, CA: Sage.

Kirk, D., Burgess-Limerick, R., Kiss, M., Lahey, J. and Penney, D. (2004). *Senior physical education: An integrated approach* (2nd edn). Champaign, IL: Human Kinetics.

Kirk, D., Penney, D., Burgess-Limerick, R., Gorely, P. and Maynard, C. A. (2002). *The reflective performer in physical education: A complete guide to A-level study.* Champaign, IL: Human Kinetics.

Knapp, M. S. and Woolverton, S. (2004). Social class and schooling. In J. A. Banks and C. A. McGee Banks (Eds), *Handbook of research on multicultural education* (pp. 656–81). San Francisco, CA: Jossey-Bass.

Kneer, M. (1986). A description of physical education instructional theory/practice gap in selected secondary schools, *Journal of Teaching in Physical Education*, 5(2), 91–106.

Kornhaber, M. L. (2004). Appropriate and inappropriate forms of testing, assessment and accountability, *Educational Policy*, 18(1), 45–70.

Langendorfer, S. J. (2001). Should the physical education grade be included in a high school student's GPA? *Journal of Physical Education, Recreation and Dance*, 72(8), 9.

Levin, H. M. (1998). Educational performance standards and the economy, *Educational Researcher*, 27(4), 4–10.

Lim, J., Pellett, H. and Pellett, T. (2009). Integrating digital video technology in the classroom, *Journal of Physical Education, Recreation and Dance*, 80(6), 40–55.

Lingard, B. (2010). Policy borrowing, policy learning: Testing times in Australian schooling, *Critical Studies in Education*, 51(2), 129–47.

Lingard, B. and Blackmore, J. (1997). The 'performative' state and the state of educational research, *Australian Educational Researcher*, 24(3), 1–22.

Lingard, B. and Mills, M. (2007). Pedagogies making a difference: Issues of social justice and inclusion, *International Journal of Inclusive Education*, 11(3), 233–44.

Lingard, B., Taylor, S. and Rawolle, S. (2005). Bourdieu and the study of educational policy: Introduction, *Journal of Education Policy*, 20(6), 663–69.

Locker, J. and Croperly, M. (2004). Anxiety, depression and self-esteem in secondary school children: An investigation into the impact of standard assessment tests (SATs) and other important school examinations, *School Psychology International*, 25(3), 333–45.

Lubienski, S. (2003). Celebrating diversity and denying disparities: A critical assessment, *Educational Researcher*, 32(8), 30–38.

Lyle, J. (2002). *Sports coaching concepts: A framework for coaches' behaviour.* Routledge, London.

Lyotard, J.-F. (1984). *The postmodern condition: A report on knowledge*, trans. B. Bennington and B. Massumi. Minneapolis: University of Minnesota Press.

MacClure, S. (1989). *Education re-formed* (2nd edn). London: Hodder & Stoughton.

McCuaig, L. and Hay, P. J. (in press). Principled pursuits of 'the good citizen' in health and physical education, *Physical Education and Sport Pedagogy*.

Macdonald, D. (2011). Like a fish in water: Physical education policy and practice in the era of neoliberal globalization, *QUEST*, 63(1), 36–45.

Macdonald, D. and Brooker, R. (1997a). Assessment issues in a performance-based subject: A case study of physical education, *Studies in Educational Evaluation*, 23(1), 83–102.

—— (1997b). Moving beyond the crises in secondary physical education: An Australian initiative, *Journal of Teaching in Physical Education*, 16(2), 155–75.

MacKreth, K. (1998). Developments in 'A' level physical education, *The British Journal of Physical Education*, 29, 16–17.

McLeod, J. and Yates, L. (2006). *Making modern lives*. Albany, NY: State University of New York Press.

McNeil, L. (2000). *Contradictions of school reform: Educational costs of standardised testing*. New York: Routledge.

MacPhail, A. and Halbert, J. (2010). 'We had to do intelligent thinking during recent PE': Students' and teachers' experiences of assessment for learning in post-primary physical education, *Assessment in Education*, 17(1), 23–39.

Markus, K. A. (1998). Science, measurement, and validity: Is completion of Samuel Messick's synthesis possible?, *Social Indicators Research*, 45(1–3), 7–34.

Matanin, M. and Tannehill, D. (1994). Assessment and grading in physical education, *Journal of Teaching in Physical Education*, 13(4), 395–405.

Meadmore, D. (2001). The pursuit of standards: Simply managing education? *International Journal of Inclusive Education*, 5(4), 353–65.

Meadmore, D. and Meadmore, P. (2004). The boundlessness of performativity in elite Australian schools, *Discourse: Studies in the Cultural Politics of Education*, 25(3), 375–87.

Memmert, D. and Harvey, S. (2008). The game performance assessment instrument (GPAI): Some concerns and solutions for further development, *Journal of Teaching in Physical Education*, 27(2), 220–40.

Messick, S. (1989). Validity. In: R. L. Linn (Ed.), *Educational measurement* (3rd edn) (pp. 13–103). Washington, DC: American Council on Education and National Council on Measurement in Education.

—— (1994). The interplay of evidence and consequences in the validation of performance assessments, *Educational Researcher*, 23(2), 13–23.

—— (1995). Standards of validity and the validity of standards in performance assessment, *Educational Measurement: Issues and Practices*, 14(4), 5–8.

—— (1998). Test validity: A matter of consequence, *Social Indicators Research*, 45(1–3), 35–44.

Ministry of Education (MoE) (2007). *Statement of Intent 2007–2012*. Wellington, New Zealand: Ministry of Education.

Mitchell, S. A., Oslin, J. L. and Griffin, L. L. (2006). *Teaching sport concepts and skills: A tactical games approach* (2nd edn). Champaign, IL: Human Kinetics.

Moore, R. (2011). Foreword. In D. Frandji and P. Vitale (Eds), *Knowledge, pedagogy and society: International perspectives in Basil Bernstein's sociology of education* (pp. xiv–xvi). London: Routledge.

Moss, P. (1998). Recovering a dialectical view of rationality, *Social Indicators Research*, 45(1–3), 55–67.

Moss, P. A., Girard, B. J. and Haniford, L. C. (2006). Validity in educational assessment, *Review of Research in Education*, 30(1), 109–62.

Nadeau, L., Richard, J.-F. and Godbout, P. (2008). The validity and reliability of a performance assessment procedure in ice hockey, *Physical Education and Sport Pedagogy*, 13(1), 65–83.

Nesbit, J. C. and Winne, P. H. (2008). Tools for learning in an information society. In T. Willoughby and E. Wood (Eds), *Children's learning in a digital world* (pp. 173–95). Maldon: Blackwell.

Nicols, R., Davis, K. L., McCord, T., Schmidt, D. and Slezak, A. M. (2009). The use of heart rate monitors in physical education, *Strategies*, 22(6), 19–23.

North, C. (2008). What is all this talk about 'social justice'? Mapping the terrain of education's latest catchphrase, *Teachers College Record*, 110(6), 1182–1206.

Office for Standards in Education (OFSTED) (1998). *Secondary education: A review of secondary schools in England 1993–97*. London: OFSTED.

Oslin, J. L. (2003). The role of assessment in teaching games for understanding. In L. L. Griffin and J. I. Butler (Eds), *Teaching Games for Understanding: Theory, research, and practice* (pp. 125–36). Champaign, IL: Human Kinetics.

Oslin, J. L., Mitchell, S. A. and Griffin, L. L. (1998). The Game Performance Assessment Inventory (GPAI): Development and preliminary validation, *Journal of Teaching in Physical Education*, 17(2), 231–43.

Pelgrum, W. J. and Plomp, T. (2004). The turtle stands on the basis of an emerging educational paradigm. In A. Aviram and J. Richardson (Eds), *Upon what does the turtle stand? Rethinking education for the digital age* (pp. 53–68). Dordrech, Netherlands: Kluwer Academic Publishers.

Penney, D. (2008). Playing a political game and playing for position: Policy and curriculum development in health and physical education, *European Physical Education Review*, 14(1), 33–49.

—— (2011). Guest editorial: Physical education and sport in schools. Policy and pedagogical perspectives, *European Physical Education Review*, 17(3), 271–72.

Penney, D. and Evans, J. (1999). *Politics, policy and practice in physical education*. London: FN Spon.

—— (2004). Levels on the playing field: Ability and inclusion in level frameworks in health and physical education. Paper presented at the Australian Association for Research in Education Conference, 28 November–2 December, Melbourne, Australia.

Penney, D. and Jess, M. (2004). Physical education and physically active lives: A lifelong approach to curriculum development. *Sport Education and Society*, 9(2), 269–88.

Penney, D. and Evans, J. (2005). Policy, power and politics in physical education. In K. Green (Ed.), *Physical education: A reader*. London: Sage Publications.

Penney, D. and Mr Walker (2007). Senior secondary schooling in Western Australia: Transforming curriculum, lives and society?, *Curriculum Perspectives*, 27(3), 22–35.

Penney, D. and Hay, P. J. (2008). Inclusivity and senior physical education: Insights from Queensland and Western Australia, *Sport, Education and Society*, 13(4), 431–52.

Penney, D., Macdonald, D. and Kirk, D. (1997). A new physical education? Paper prepared for Annual Conference of Australian Association for Research in Education, 30 November–4 December, Brisbane, Australia.

Penney, D., Kinchin, G. and Quill, M. (2005). Assessment and sport education. In D. Penney, G. Clarke, M. Quill and G. Kinchin (Eds), *Sport education in physical education: Research based practice* (pp. 55–70). London: Routledge.

Penney, D., Brooker, R., Hay, P. and Gillespie, L. (2009). Curriculum, pedagogy and assessment: Three message systems of schooling and dimensions of quality physical education, *Sport, Education and Society*, 14(4), 421–42.

Penney, D., Jones, A., Newhouse, P. and Cambell, A. (2011). Developing a digital assessment in senior secondary physical education, *Physical Education and Sport Pedagogy*, DOI: 10.1080/17408989.2011.582490.

Penney, D., Gillespie, L., Jones, A., Newhouse, P. and Cambell, A. (2011). Assessment in senior secondary physical education: Questions of judgement. In G. Dodd (Ed.), *Edited proceedings of the 27th ACHPER international conference* (pp. 103–10). Adelaide, S.A.: ACHPER. (Retrieved from <www.achper.org.au/conferences-events/2011-conference-proceedings>).

Petrie, K. and lisahunter. (2011). Primary teachers, policy, and physical education, *European Physical Education Review*, 17(3), 325–39.

Popham, W. J. (2006). Needed: A dose of assessment literacy, *Educational Leadership*, 63(6), 84–85.

—— (2009). Assessment literacy for teachers: Faddish or fundamental? *Theory into Practice*, 48, 4–11.

Popkewitz, T. S. (1999). Critical traditions, modernisms, and the 'posts'. In T. S. Popkewitz and L. Fendler (Eds), *Critical theories in education: Changing terrains of knowledge and politics* (pp. 1–13). New York, Routledge.

Queensland Studies Authority (QSA) (2010). *Physical education: Senior syllabus 2010*. Brisbane, Australia: Queensland Studies Authority.

Ranson, S. (2003). Public accountability in the age of neo-liberal governance, *Journal of Education Policy*, 18(5), 459–80.

Reay, D. and Wiliam, D. (1999). 'I'll be a nothing': Structure, agency and the construction of identity through assessment, *British Educational Research Journal*, 25(3), 343–54.

Redelius, K. and Hay, P. J. (2009). Defining, acquiring and transacting cultural capital through assessment in physical education. *European Physical Education Review*, 15(3), 275–94.

—— (2011). Student views on criterion-referenced assessment and grading in Swedish physical education, *Physical Education and Sport Pedagogy*, DOI: 10.1080/17408989.2010.548064.

Richardson, T. and Johanningmeier, E. V. (1997). Intelligence testing: The legitimation of a meritocratic educational science, *International Journal of Educational Research*, 27(8), 699–714.

Rink, J. and Mitchell, M. (2002). High stakes assessment: A journey into unknown territory, *Quest*, 54(3), 205–23.

Rizvi, F. and Lingard, B. (2010). *Globalizing education policy*. London: Routledge.

Rovai, A. P. (2004). A constructivist approach to online college learning, *Internet and Higher Education*, 7, 79–93.

Rynne, S., Mallett, C. and Tinning, R., (2009). High performance coaching: Institutes of sport as sites for learning, *International Journal of Sport Science and Coaching*, 1, 223–34.

Sadler, D. R. (1998). Formative assessment: Revisiting the territory, *Assessment in Education*, 5(1), 77–84.

——(2005). Interpretations of criteria-based assessment and grading in higher education, *Assessment and Evaluation in Higher Education*, 30(2), 175–94.

Shepard, L. (2000). The role of assessment in a learning culture, *Educational Researcher*, 29(7), 4–14.

Shilling, C. (1993). *The body and social theory*. London: Sage.

—— (2004). Physical capital and situated action: A new direction for corporeal sociology, *British Journal of Sociology of Education*, 25(4), 473–87.

Siedentop, D. (1994). *Sport education: Quality PE through positive sport experiences*. Champaign, IL: Human Kinetics.

Siedentop, D., Hastie, P. A. and van der Mars, H. (2004). *Complete guide to sport education*. Champaign, IL: Human Kinetics.

Simon, B. (1988). *Bending the rules: The Baker 'reform' of education*. London: Lawrence & Wishart.

Skolverket (2002). *Idrott och hälsa* (Physical education and health: The Swedish syllabus for the nine-year compulsory school) (for the English version, <www.skolverket.se>).

Smyth, J. and Shacklock, G. (1998). *Remaking teaching: Ideology, policy and practice.* London: Routledge.

Smyth, J., Dow, A., Hattam, R., Reid, A. and Shacklock, G. (2000). *Teachers' work in a globalizing economy.* London: Falmer Press.

Staiano, A. E. and Calvert, S. L. (2011). Exergames for physical education courses: Physical, social, and cognitive benefits, *Child Development Perspectives,* 5(2), 93–98.

Sternberg, R. J. (1998). Abilities are forms of developing expertise, *Educational Researcher,* 27(3), 11–20.

Stiggins, R. J. (1991). Assessment literacy, *Phi Delta Kappan,* 72(7), 534–39.

—— (1999). Evaluating classroom assessment training in teacher education programs. *Educational Measurement: Issues and Practice,* 18(1), 23–27.

Stobart, G. (2005). Fairness in multicultural assessment systems, *Assessment in Education,* 12(3), 275–87.

—— (2008). *Testing times: The uses and abuses of assessment.* London: Routledge.

Taggart, A., Browne, T. and Alexander, K. (1995). Three schools' approaches to assessment in sport education, *The ACHPER Healthy Lifestyles Journal,* 42(4), 12–15.

Taras, M. (2002). Using assessment for learning and learning from assessment, *Assessment & Evaluation in Higher Education,* 27(6), 501–10.

Taylor, L. (2009). Developing assessment literacy, *Annual Review of Applied Linguistics,* 29, 21–36.

Teese, R. (1998). Curriculum hierarchy, private schooling, and the segmentation of Australian secondary education, 1947–85, *British Journal of Sociology of Education,* 19(3), 401–17.

—— (2000). *Academic success and social power: Examinations and inequality.* Carlton South, Australia: Melbourne University Press.

Teese, R. and Polesel, J. (2003). *Undemocratic schooling: Equity and quality in mass secondary education in Australia.* Carlton South, Australia: Melbourne University Press.

Terwilliger, J. (1997). Semantics, psychometrics, and assessment reform: A close look at 'authentic' assessment, *Educational Researcher,* 26(8), 24–27.

Thorburn, M. (2007). Achieving conceptual and curriculum coherence in high-stakes school examinations in physical education, *Physical Education and Sport Pedagogy,* 12(2), 163–84.

Thorburn, M. and Collins, D. (2003). Integrated curriculum models and their effects on teachers' pedagogy practices, *European Physical Education Review,* 9(2), 185–209.

Thorpe, R., Bunker, D. and Almond, L. (Eds). (1986). *Rethinking games teaching.* Loughborough: Department of PE and Sports Science, University of Loughborough.

Tinning, R. (2000). Seeking a realistic contribution: Considering physical education within HPE in New Zealand and Australia, *Journal of Physical Education New Zealand,* 33(3), 8–21.

—— (2009). Pedagogy, sport pedagogy, and the field of kinesiology, *Quest,* 60(3), 405–24.

Tsangaridou, N. and O'Sullivan, M. (1997). The role of reflection in shaping physical education teachers' educational values and practices, *Journal of Teaching in Physical Education,* 17(1), 2–25.

Varvel, V. E., Montague, R. and Estabrook, L. S. (2007). Policy and e-learning. In R. Andrews and C. Haythornthwaite (Eds), *The Sage handbook of e-learning research* (pp. 269–85). London: Sage.

Veal, M.-L. (1988). Pupil assessment practices and perceptions of secondary teachers, *Journal of Teaching in Physical Education,* 7(4), 327–42.

—— (1995). Assessment as an instructional tool, *Strategies,* 8(6), 10–15.

Wacquant, L. (1989). Towards a reflexive sociology: A workshop with Pierre Bourdieu, *Sociological Theory*, 7(1), 26–63.

Wallhead, T. and O'Sullivan, M. (2005). Sport Education: Physical education for the new millennium?, *Physical Education and Sport Pedagogy*, 10(2), 181–210.

Watson, L. (2003). *Lifelong learning in Australia*. Canberra: Commonwealth of Australia.

Webb, J., Schirato, T. and Danaher, G. (2002). *Understanding Bourdieu*. Crows Nest: Allen & Unwin.

Welsh Joint Examination Committee (WJEC) (2008). *GCE examinations from 2009. First AS award: Summer 2009. First A level award: Summer 2010. Physical education.* Cardiff: WJEC. (Retrieved from <www.wjec.co.uk/index.php?subject=94& level=21>).

West, L. (2004). The trouble with lifelong learning. In D. Hayes (Ed.), *The Routledge Falmer guide to key debates in education* (pp. 138–41). London: RoutledgeFalmer.

Wright, J. and Burrows, L. (2006). Re-conceiving ability in physical education: A social analysis, *Sport, Education and Society*, 11(3), 275–92.

Index